TEACHER'S MANUAL AND ACHIEVEMENT TESTS

NorthStar 1

READING AND WRITING

SECOND EDITION

AUTHOR

John Beaumont

SERIES EDITORS

Frances Boyd

Carol Numrich

PEARSON

Longman

NorthStar: Reading and Writing Level 1, Second Edition
Teacher's Manual and Achievement Tests

Pearson Education, 10 Bank Street, White Plains, NY 10606

Teacher's Manual by Robin Mills. Activities for secondary schools by Ann Hilborn and Linda Riehl.

Achievement Tests developed by Dr. Joan Jamieson and Dr. Carol Chapelle.

Achievement Tests by Tony Becker and Dana Klinek.

Staff credits: The people who made up the **NorthStar: Reading and Writing Level 1, Second Edition Teacher's Manual** team, representing editorial, production, design, and manufacturing, are Dave Dickey, Christine Edmonds, Ann France, Gosia Jaros-White, Dana Klinek, Françoise Leffler, Melissa Leyva, Sherry Preiss, Robert Ruvo, Debbie Sistino, Kathleen Smith, Paula Van Ells, and Adina Zoltan.

Cover Art: Silvia Rojas/Getty Images
Text composition: ElectraGraphics, Inc.
Text font: 11.5/13 Minion

ISBN-10: 0-13-233643-X
ISBN-13: 978-0-13-233643-7

PEARSON LONGMAN ON THE WEB

Pearsonlongman.com offers online resources for teachers and students. Access our Companion Websites, our online catalog, and our local offices around the world.

Visit us at **www.pearsonlongman.com**.

Printed in the United States of America
2 3 4 5 6 7 8 9 10—HAM—13 12 11 10 09

CONTENTS

UNIT-BY-UNIT TEACHING SUGGESTIONS

ACHIEVEMENT TESTS

WELCOME TO NORTHSTAR

SECOND EDITION

NorthStar, now in a new edition, motivates students to succeed in their **academic** as well as **personal** language goals.

For each of the five levels, the two strands—*Reading and Writing* and *Listening and Speaking*—provide a fully integrated approach for students and teachers.

WHAT IS SPECIAL ABOUT THE NEW EDITION?

NEW THEMES

New themes and **updated content**—presented in a **variety of genres**, including literature and lectures, and in **authentic reading and listening selections**—challenge students intellectually.

ACADEMIC SKILLS

More purposeful **integration of critical thinking** and an enhanced focus on **academic skills** such as inferencing, synthesizing, note taking, and test taking help students develop strategies for **success** in the **classroom** and on **standardized tests**. A **culminating productive task** galvanizes content, language, and **critical thinking skills**.

➤ In the *Reading and Writing* strand, a new, **fully integrated writing section** leads students through the **writing process** with engaging writing assignments focusing on various rhetorical modes.

➤ In the *Listening and Speaking* strand, a **structured approach** gives students opportunities for **more extended and creative oral practice**, for example, presentations, simulations, debates, case studies, and public service announcements.

NEW DESIGN

Full **color pages** with more **photos, illustrations, and graphic organizers** foster student engagement and make the content and activities come alive.

MyNorthStarLab

MyNorthStarLab, an easy-to-use **online learning and assessment program**, offers:

➤ Unlimited access to reading and listening selections and DVD segments.

➤ Focused test preparation to help students succeed on international exams such as TOEFL® and IELTS®. Pre- and post-unit assessments improve results by providing individualized instruction, instant feedback, and personalized study plans.

➤ Original activities that support and extend the *NorthStar* program. These include pronunciation practice using voice recording tools, and activities to build note taking skills and academic vocabulary.

➤ Tools that save time. These include a flexible gradebook and authoring features that give teachers control of content and help them track student progress.

THE NORTHSTAR APPROACH

The *NorthStar* series is based on **current research in language acquisition** and on the **experiences of teachers and curriculum designers**. Five principles guide the *NorthStar* approach.

PRINCIPLES

1   The more profoundly students are stimulated intellectually and emotionally, the more language they will use and retain.

The thematic organization of *NorthStar* promotes intellectual and emotional stimulation. The 50 sophisticated themes in *NorthStar* present intriguing topics such as recycled fashion, restorative justice, personal carbon footprints, and microfinance. The authentic content engages students, links them to language use outside of the classroom, and encourages personal expression and critical thinking.

2   Students can learn both the form and content of the language.

Grammar, vocabulary, and culture are inextricably woven into the units, providing students with systematic and multiple exposures to language forms in a variety of contexts. As the theme is developed, students can express complex thoughts using a higher level of language.

3   Successful students are active learners.

Tasks are designed to be creative, active, and varied. Topics are interesting and up-to-date. Together these tasks and topics (1) allow teachers to bring the outside world into the classroom and (2) motivate students to apply their classroom learning in the outside world.

4   Students need feedback.

This feedback comes naturally when students work together practicing language and participating in open-ended opinion and inference tasks. Whole class activities invite teachers' feedback on the spot or via audio/video recordings or notes. The innovative new MyNorthStarLab gives students immediate feedback as they complete computer-graded language activities online; it also gives students the opportunity to submit writing or speaking assignments electronically to their instructor for feedback later.

5   The quality of relationships in the language classroom is important because students are asked to express themselves on issues and ideas.

The information and activities in *NorthStar* promote genuine interaction, acceptance of differences, and authentic communication. By building skills and exploring ideas, the exercises help students participate in discussions and write essays of an increasingly complex and sophisticated nature.

THE NORTHSTAR UNIT

FOCUS ON THE TOPIC

This section introduces students to the unifying theme
of the reading selections.

> **PREDICT** and **SHARE INFORMATION** foster interest in the unit topic and help
> students develop a personal connection to it.
>
> **BACKGROUND AND VOCABULARY** activities provide students with tools for
> understanding the first reading selection. Later in the unit, students review
> this vocabulary and learn related idioms, collocations, and word forms. This
> helps them explore content and expand their written and spoken language.

UNIT
3
Art for Everyone

FOCUS ON THE TOPIC

A PREDICT

Look at the picture. Discuss the questions with the class.

1. What is the man doing?
2. Where is he?
3. Do you know this man?

43

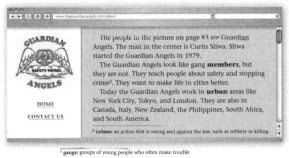

B SHARE INFORMATION

Read the list of social issues. Are these problems for young people in your city or
town? Rate each social issue from **1** (not a problem) to **4** (a serious problem).
Circle the number. Discuss your answers with the class.

SOCIAL ISSUES	Not a Problem			A Serious Problem
1. Alcohol	1	2	3	4
2. Drugs	1	2	3	4
3. Not finding a job	1	2	3	4
4. Gangs[1]	1	2	3	4
5. Having babies	1	2	3	4
6. Smoking	1	2	3	4
7. Not staying in school	1	2	3	4
8. Your idea _____:	1	2	3	4

C BACKGROUND AND VOCABULARY

1 Read the information about the Guardian Angels.

www.theguardianangels.com/about

GUARDIAN
SAFETY PATROL
ANGELS

HOME

CONTACT US

The people in the picture on page 83 are Guardian
Angels. The man in the center is Curtis Sliwa. Sliwa
started the Guardian Angels in 1979.

The Guardian Angels look like gang **members**, but
they are not. They teach people about safety and stopping
crime[2]. They want to make life in cities better.

Today the Guardian Angels work in **urban** areas like
New York City, Tokyo, and London. They are also in
Canada, Italy, New Zealand, the Philippines, South Africa,
and South America.

[2] **crime:** an action that is wrong and against the law, such as robbery or killing.

[1] **gangs:** groups of young people who often make trouble

84   UNIT 5

② FOCUS ON READING

This section focuses on understanding two contrasting reading selections.

> **READING ONE** is a literary selection, academic article, news piece, blog, or other genre that addresses the unit topic. In levels 1 to 3, readings are based on authentic materials. In levels 4 and 5, all the readings are authentic.
>
> **READ FOR MAIN IDEAS** and **READ FOR DETAILS** are comprehension activities that lead students to an understanding and appreciation of the first selection.

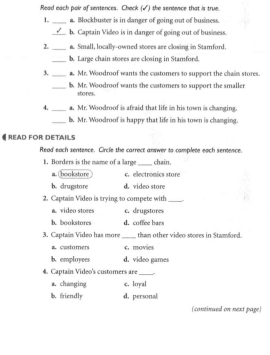

② FOCUS ON READING

Ⓐ READING ONE: A Letter from the Principal

Read only the first sentence of Mr. Collins' letter. Then check (✓) the **true** sentence.

____ Mr. Collins is asking students and parents about a school uniform.

____ Mr. Collins is telling students and parents about a uniform.

LINCOLN HIGH SCHOOL

Mr. Peter F. Collins
Principal
Lincoln High School
2064 School Street
Salem, New Hampshire 03079

Dear Students and Parents:

Next year, all students at Lincoln High School will wear a school uniform.

Boys and girls will wear a white shirt and a dark blue jacket. Boys will also wear a blue tie and dark gray pants. Girls will wear dark gray pants or a dark gray skirt.

Wearing a uniform is a good idea. The uniform will help students study hard. They will think about school and school work, not about **fashion**. Today, students think too much about **clothes** and how they look. It is important to think about education first.

Uniforms also look **neat** and clean. When students are neat and clean, they are more **comfortable**. When they are more comfortable, they study more.

Uniforms will also **increase** school **spirit**. Students in uniforms will look like a team, and they will work together as a team.

Uniforms are also less **expensive** than popular **designer** clothes. Parents will be happy about that. Parents can buy the new school uniform at Benson's Department Store on Broadway in the Salem Shopping Center.

Enjoy your summer vacation.

Sincerely,

Peter F. Collins

Peter F. Collins

What Will I Wear? **29**

◀ READ FOR MAIN IDEAS

Read each pair of sentences. Check (✓) the sentence that is true.

1. ____ **a.** Blockbuster is in danger of going out of business.

   _✓_ **b.** Captain Video is in danger of going out of business.

2. ____ **a.** Small, locally-owned stores are closing in Stamford.

   ____ **b.** Large chain stores are closing in Stamford.

3. ____ **a.** Mr. Woodroof wants the customers to support the chain stores.

   ____ **b.** Mr. Woodroof wants the customers to support the smaller stores.

4. ____ **a.** Mr. Woodroof is afraid that life in his town is changing.

   ____ **b.** Mr. Woodroof is happy that life in his town is changing.

◀ READ FOR DETAILS

Read each sentence. Circle the correct answer to complete each sentence.

1. Borders is the name of a large ____ chain.

   a. bookstore   **c.** electronics store

   b. drugstore   **d.** video store

2. Captain Video is trying to compete with ____.

   a. video stores   **c.** drugstores

   b. bookstores   **d.** coffee bars

3. Captain Video has more ____ than other video stores in Stamford.

   a. customers   **c.** movies

   b. employees   **d.** video games

4. Captain Video's customers are ____.

   a. changing   **c.** loyal

   b. friendly   **d.** personal

(continued on next page)

Going Out of Business? **113**

> Following this comprehension section, the **MAKE INFERENCES** activity prompts students to "read between the lines," move beyond the literal meaning, exercise critical thinking skills, and understand the text on a more academic level. Students follow up with pair or group work to discuss topics in the **EXPRESS OPINIONS** section.

READING TWO offers another perspective on the topic and usually belongs to another genre. Again, in levels 1 to 3, the readings are based on authentic materials, and in levels 4 and 5, they are authentic. This second reading is followed by an activity that challenges students to question ideas they formed about the first reading, and to use appropriate language skills to analyze and explain their ideas.

INTEGRATE READINGS ONE AND TWO presents culminating activities. Students are challenged to take what they have learned, organize the information, and synthesize it in a meaningful way. Students practice skills that are essential for success in authentic academic settings and on standardized tests.

B **READING TWO: Bram Tarek**

1 *Read the imaginary interview with Bram Tarek.*

Bram Tarek:
Young Basketball
Star Says "No"
to the Pros

Interview by
Nicola Quinn

You probably don't know Bram Tarek—not yet. But basketball coaches know him, and they think he has a lot of talent. He is a college basketball star. At 18 years old and after graduating from high school, Bram Tarek is now old enough to join a professional basketball team, but the NBA[1] will have to wait. Tarek wants to graduate from college first.

NQ: Bram, everyone expected you to join the NBA this year. Why did you decide to finish college first?

BT: Well, I planned to join the NBA as soon as I was old enough. But then I met

older basketball players. They said I should stay in college.

NQ: Who did you talk to?

BT: Several basketball players. But Kareem Abdul-Jabbar probably helped me the most. He is my biggest basketball hero. He's the greatest. But, in his day, all players had to go to college before joining the NBA. Today it's different. He said college helped the players to become more mature—intellectually and physically.

NQ: But what about the money? How can you say "no" to all that money?

BT: Oh, that was really hard! On the wall in my bedroom, I had photos of all the beautiful cars I wanted to buy!

NQ: So, what happened?

BT: Kareem helped a lot. He really taught me that money is not #1. The important things in life are family, education, and health. And I still have a lot to learn.

NQ: What exactly do you need to learn?

BT: I need to learn more about working with other people—especially with people I don't agree with. I want to be a leader like Kareem. Thirty years from now, I want people to say "Bram Tarek was—or is—a great athlete, a great leader, and a good person," not "Bram Tarek was a great athlete with a lot of expensive cars when he was 18."

[1] **NBA:** National Basketball Association. All professional basketball teams in the U.S. are in the NBA.

C **INTEGRATE READINGS ONE AND TWO**

STEP 1: Organize

Think about New York's problems in Reading Two and the solutions in Reading One. Which solutions might work for each problem? Write the solutions from the box in the chart. More than one answer is possible.

| bike lanes | helicopter | sky train | tunnel under city |
| Deduct-a-Ride | online traffic map | traffic tax | |

TRAFFIC PROBLEMS IN NEW YORK CITY	POSSIBLE SOLUTIONS
Trucks	
Poor conditions of roads and bridges	
Streets not safe for pedestrians	
Streets not safe for bicyclists	
Slow buses	
Pollution, including noise	

STEP 2: Synthesize

1 *Work with a partner. One student is Rafael Torres, and the other is the mayor of New York. Complete the interview between Torres (T) and the mayor (M). Use the information from the readings. Do not give your own opinion.*

T: Mr. Mayor, as you know, there are serious traffic problems in this city. I have data to show you.

M: Yes, I know. What did the poll say?

T: Well, one big problem is . . .

M: OK, to solve that problem I want to . . .

2 *Change roles and repeat Exercise 1 with a different problem and solution.*

3 *Present one of your conversations to the class.*

---

③ FOCUS ON WRITING

This section emphasizes development of productive skills for writing. It includes sections on vocabulary, grammar, and the writing process.

The **VOCABULARY** section leads students from reviewing the unit vocabulary, to practicing and expanding their use of it, and then working with it—using it creatively in both this section and in the final writing task.

Students learn useful structures for writing in the **GRAMMAR** section, which offers a concise presentation and targeted practice. Vocabulary items are recycled here, providing multiple exposures leading to mastery. For additional practice with the grammar presented, students and teachers can consult the GRAMMAR BOOK REFERENCES at the end of the book for corresponding material in the *Focus on Grammar* and Azar series.

---

③ FOCUS ON WRITING

Ⓐ VOCABULARY

◀ REVIEW

Read the paragraph. Then fill in the blanks with words from the box.

advice	laughed	quotes
chat	meet	safe
community	peace	users
goal	personal	volunteers

At 16, Bronwyn Polson's _____goal_____ was to do something good for her
1.
_____ and for the world. Bronwyn called newspapers and social service
2.
organizations, but they just _____. They said she was too young to help.
3.
So, she started a website called The Friendship Page. She believes in
"_____ through friendship." On The Friendship Page people
4.
_____ new friends. They can _____ about important things.
5.   6.
It has _____ for people with friendship problems. The _____
7.   8.
page is the most popular part.
_____ help Bronwyn. They want The Friendship Page to be
9.
_____ for everyone. _____ do not give important
10.   11.
_____ information. The Friendship Page is a lot of work, but Bronwyn
12.
enjoys it very much.

Ⓑ GRAMMAR: Pronouns and Possessive Adjectives

1 *Read the paragraph. Look at the underlined words. Draw an arrow from each underlined word to the noun it refers to. Then answer the questions.*

What Do Urban Angels Do?

Urban Angels have many activities after school and on Saturdays. They go on trips to local museums and to other places outside the city. They also visit businesses to learn about different jobs. Most important, Urban Angels help out in their community. At "park clean-ups" they go to city parks and make them beautiful again.

1. Which underlined word is a subject?
2. Which underlined word is an object?
3. Which underlined word shows possession?

PRONOUNS AND POSSESSIVE ADJECTIVES

A **pronoun** is a word that takes the place of a noun. Pronouns are useful when you don't want to repeat a noun in a sentence.	[subject] **Urban Angels** have many activities.
1. Subject pronouns take the place of the subject in a sentence. Subject pronouns include: *I, you, he, she, it, we, and they.*	[subject / pronoun] **They** go on trips to local museums. **You** can become an Urban Angel.
2. Object pronouns take the place of an object. Objects usually come after the verb. Object pronouns also come after prepositions like *for, to, and from.* Object pronouns include: *me, you, him, her, it, us, and them.*	[object] Urban Angels like to help **people**. [object pronoun] Urban Angels teach **them** about safety. The Urban Angels program needs **support**. New York City helps pay for **it**.
3. Possessive adjectives are like pronouns. They show possession or ownership. They always come before a noun. Possessive adjectives include: *my, your, his, her, its, our, and their.*	Urban Angels help out in **their** community. **My** goal is to be a fashion designer. Kelly isn't an Urban Angel, but **her** friend is.

The **WRITING** section of each unit leads students through the writing process and presents a challenging and imaginative writing task that directs students to integrate the content, vocabulary, and grammar from the unit.

- Students practice a short **pre-writing strategy**, such as freewriting, clustering, brainstorming, interviewing, listing, making a chart or diagram, categorizing, or classifying.

- Then students organize their ideas and write, using a **specific structural or rhetorical pattern** that fits the subject at hand.

- Students then learn **revising techniques** within a sentence-level or paragraph-level activity to help them move towards **coherence and unity** in their writing.

C WRITING

In this unit, you read a timeline and an interview about Keith Haring. You also looked at examples of Keith Haring's art.

You are going to **write a biography about Keith Haring.** A **biography** is a story of a person's life. Use the vocabulary and grammar from the unit.*

◀ PREPARE TO WRITE: Finding Information in a Reading

To help you plan your biography, you are going to **look for information in the readings** in this unit as a prewriting activity.

1 *Look at the timeline on page 47. Then answer the questions about Keith Haring.*

1. Where was Keith Haring born?

   Keith Haring was born in Kutztown, Pennsylvania.

2. When was Keith Haring born?

   _____

3. When was Haring arrested by the police? Why?

   _____

4. When and where was Haring an art student?

   _____

5. What were his first drawings? Where were they?

   _____

6. When and where was Haring's first important art show?

   _____

2 *Look at Reading One on pages 48–49. Find one more idea about Keith Haring that you think is interesting. Write it on the line. Use this information in your biography, too.*

   _____

---

*For Alternative Writing Topics, see page 64. These topics can be used in place of the writing topic for this unit or as homework. The alternative topics relate to the theme of the unit, but may not target the same grammar or rhetorical structures taught in the unit.

◀ REVISE: Ordering Your Ideas

A group of sentences about one main idea is a **paragraph**.

Read the paragraphs. Then answer the questions.

> The Friendship Page is very safe. The volunteers watch the website carefully. They want it to be safe for everyone, especially for young people. We talk to the Australian police about Internet safety, too.

How many sentences are in this paragraph? _____

> MySpace started in 2003. Today, more than 100 million people from more than 14 countries use MySpace. Most users are 16–54 years old. They must be 14 years or older, but it is difficult to check. Forty-nine percent of MySpace users are female and 51 percent are male. There are more than 50,000 interesting groups, like health, sports, music, and TV.

How many sentences are in this paragraph? _____

When you write your paragraph, you can organize the information in different ways. Here are two: (1) person by person or (2) by ideas. Look at Description One and Description Two.

1 *Read Description One. It gives sentences about Fernando and then sentences about his friend, Ricardo. The order is "person by person."*

Description One

> My classmate's name is Fernando. He is from Spain. He is 21 years old. He is a student in Chicago. Fernando is friendly. He likes going to parties. Fernando's best friend is Ricardo. He is from Spain. He is 20 years old. He is a student in Madrid. Ricardo is friendly and athletic. He likes going to parties and playing sports.

In the final phase of the writing process, students **edit** their work with the help of a **checklist** that focuses on mechanics, completeness, enhancing style, and incorporating the vocabulary and grammar from the unit.

ALTERNATIVE WRITING TOPICS are provided at the end of the unit. They can be used as *alternatives* to the final writing task, or as *additional* assignments. RESEARCH TOPICS tied to the theme of the unit are organized in a special section at the back of the book.

MyNorthStarLab

MyNorthStarLab supports students with **individualized instruction**, **feedback**, and **extra help**. A wide array of resources, including a flexible **gradebook**, helps teachers manage student progress.

The MyNorthStarLab **WELCOME** page **organizes assignments and grades**, and **facilitates communication** between students and teachers.

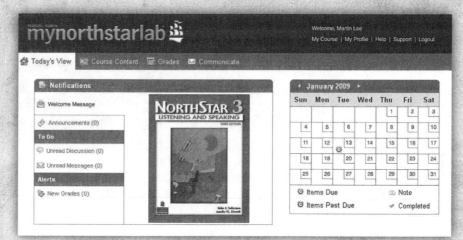

For each unit, MyNorthStarLab provides a **READINESS CHECK**.

➤ Activities **assess** student knowledge **before** beginning the unit and **follow up** with individualized instruction.

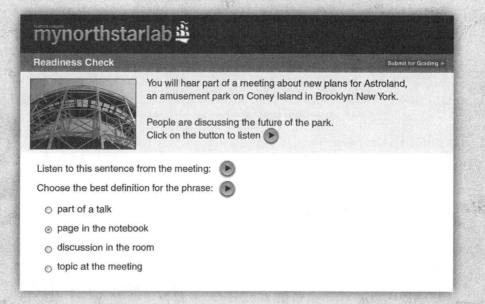

Student book material and **new** practice activities are available to students online.

➢ Students benefit from virtually unlimited **practice anywhere, anytime**.

Interaction with **Internet** and **video** materials will:

➢ Expand students' knowledge of the topic.

➢ Help students practice new vocabulary and grammar.

INTEGRATED SKILL ACTIVITIES in MyNorthStarLab challenge students to bring together the **language skills** and **critical thinking skills** that they have practiced throughout the unit.

The MyNorthStarLab **ASSESSMENT** tools allow instructors to customize and deliver achievement tests online.

mynorthstarlab

Integrated Task • Read, Listen, Write   Submit for Grading ▶

THE ADVENTURE OF A LIFETIME

READ, LISTEN AND WRITE ABOUT TOURISM IN ANTARCTICA
Read.
Read the text. Then answer the question.

According to the text, how can tourism benefit the Antarctic?

We at the Antarctic Travel Society encourage you to consider an excited guided tour of Antarctica for your next vacation.

The Antarctic Travel society carefully plans and operates tours of the Antarctic by ship. There are three trips per day leaving from ports in South America and Australia. Each ship carries only about 100 passengers at a time. Tours run from November through March to the ice-free areas along the coast of Antarctica.

In addition to touring the coast, our ships stop for on-land visits, which generally last for about three hours. Activities include guided sightseeing, mountain climbing, camping, kayaking, and scuba diving. For a longer stay, camping trips can also be arranged.

Our tours will give you an opportunity to experience the richness of Antarctica, including its wildlife, history, active research stations, and, most of all, its natural beauty.

Tours are supervised by the ship's staff. The staff generally includes experts in animal and sea life and other Antarctica specialists. There is generally one staff member for every 10 to 20 passengers. Theses trained and responsible individuals will help to make your visit to Antarctica safe, educational, and unforgettable.

Listen.
Click on the Play button and listen to the passage.
Use the outline to take notes as you listen.

Main idea:

Seven things that scientists study:

The effects of tourism:

Write.
Write about the potential and risks in Antarctica.
Follow the steps to prepare.

Step 1
• Review the text and your outline from the listening task.
• Write notes about the benefits and risks of tourism.

Step 2
Write for 20 minutes. Leave 5 minutes to edit your work.

mynorthstarlab   Welcome, Martin Lab.
                                  My Course | My Profile | Help | Support | Logout

🔍 Student Course > Achievement Test
To begin, open the Skills Check. After you submit the test, you will return to this screen. If you
will be assigned study material to help with your learning.

Skills Check   **Study Material**
Vocabulary   Part 2: Vocabulary
                            Pass Criteria: 75%
Your score: 72%
                            Name
                            ☑ Vocabulary: Exercise 1
                            ☑ Vocabulary: Exercise 2

Vocabulary Exercise 1
Click on the box next to the vocabulary word
to match its definition.

1) controversy

   an argument about opposing opinions
   protect something from harm
   a cultural practice or custom
   a small community of houses
   a park where living animals are kept
   a reminder of a place visited

2) zoo

   Hints   Hint 1

mynorthstarlab

Your Score: 80%

Listen to the beginning of a news report about Thailand.
Choose the best prediction of what the news report will contain.
There is only one right answer.

✗ ● information about religious holidays

○ information about celebrating elephants

○ information about tourist travel

○ information about the national flag

Answer(s):   information about celebrating elephants
Feedback: The speaker says:
               One might wonder—why celebrate a holiday
               in honor of the elephant?
               Click on the audio button to listen. 🔊

OVERVIEW OF THE TEACHER'S MANUAL AND ACHIEVEMENT TESTS

The *NorthStar Teacher's Manual* includes:

➤ Specific suggestions for teaching each unit

➤ Student Book Answer Key

➤ An alphabetized-by-unit word list of the key vocabulary items practiced in each unit

➤ Reproducible Achievement Tests with Answer Keys

UNIT-BY-UNIT TEACHING SUGGESTIONS

Unit-by-unit overview (scope and sequence), list of skills practiced in each section of the student book, suggested teaching times, teaching suggestions, suggestions on how to use *NorthStar* in secondary classes, Expansion/Homework activities, cross-references to the companion strand, techniques and instructions for using MyNorthStarLab

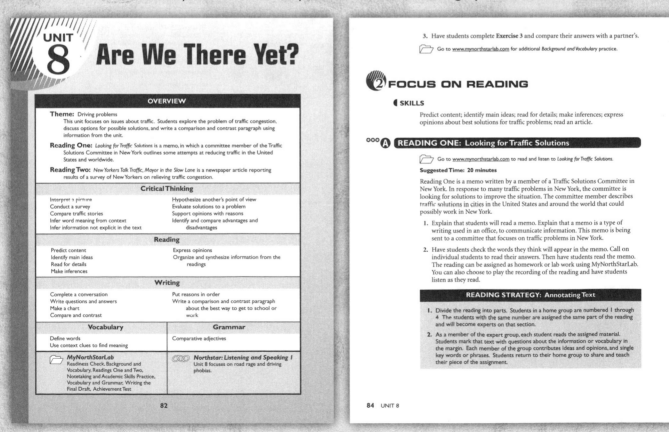

USING *NORTHSTAR* IN SECONDARY CLASSES

Each unit of the *Teacher's Manual* offers a set of strategies that provide opportunities for greater differentiation in a typical mixed classroom to meet the needs of multi-level secondary students. These strategies are equally beneficial in academic and adult classes. The scaffolded instruction enables teachers to facilitate student mastery of complex skills and ideas. Repeated exposure to concepts helps accelerate English language learning.

Reading/Listening Strategies give teachers additional support to guide students who have limited experience with basic reading/listening skills as they learn to explore and understand academic content. Suggestions are given to help students understand how to predict, determine main idea and supporting details, navigate and comprehend a text, monitor their understanding, and organize information.

Reaching All Students are activity suggestions for two levels of language proficiency, intended to assist less proficient students and challenge students with higher proficiencies. These are generally included in the Reading/Listening section to help teachers to modify reading/listening activities.

Critical Thinking suggestions focus on a hierarchy of questions using Bloom's taxonomy. These are designed specifically to scaffold questions to move students from knowledge-based questions to higher order thinking.

Vocabulary Expansion builds upon vocabulary introduced in each unit to help students further integrate vocabulary. The expansion activities are offered as word analyses or as vocabulary strategies to reinforce vocabulary skills and provide opportunities for review.

COURSE PLANNERS

Each unit contains approximately eight hours of classroom material, plus expansion, homework, and support material, including MyNorthStarLab. Teachers can customize the units by assigning some exercises for homework and/or eliminating others. To help teachers customize the units for their specific teaching situation, the unit-by-unit teaching suggestions in the *Teacher's Manual* include 1, 2, or 3 stars to indicate the relative importance of each section or exercise as follows:

✪✪✪ **Essential:** Predict, Background and Vocabulary, Reading One, Read for Main Ideas, Read for Details, Make Inferences, Express Opinions, Reading Two, Integrate Readings One and Two, Prepare to Write, Write, Revise, Edit

✪✪ **Recommended:** Share Information, Expand, Grammar

✪ **Optional:** Review, Create, Writing Topics, Research Topics

Class time available per unit	Sections to complete
8 hours or more	Essential (✪✪✪), Recommended (✪✪), Optional (✪)
6 hours	Essential (✪✪✪), Recommended (✪✪)
4 hours	Essential (✪✪✪) only

For more detailed, downloadable unit-by-unit course planners, visit www.mynorthstarlab.com or www.longman.com/northstar.

ACHIEVEMENT TESTS

The reproducible Achievement Tests allow teachers to evaluate students' progress and to identify areas where students might have problems developing their reading and writing skills. The Achievement Tests should be given upon completion of the corresponding unit.

Description

There are four parts for every test:

Parts 1 and **2** test students' receptive skills. Part 1 assesses students' mastery of reading comprehension. Part 2 assesses the knowledge of the vocabulary introduced in the unit. **Parts 3** and **4** test students' productive skills. Part 3 assesses students' knowledge of the grammar and style introduced in the unit. Part 4 is a writing test related to the content of the unit.

Administration

All parts of each test should be taken in class and students should not be allowed access to any *NorthStar* materials or to their dictionaries. Students should be able to complete Parts 1–3 within 30 minutes and Part 4 within 20 minutes.

Teachers can decide how to incorporate Part 4 (the writing task) into their testing situations. Some teachers will assign each writing task immediately after students complete Parts 1–3; others may decide to set aside another time to complete it.

Scoring the Parts

Parts 1–3: Individual test items are worth one point, for a maximum total of 30 points per test. A student's raw score can be obtained by adding together the number of correct items, or by subtracting the total number of incorrect items from 30. To convert the raw score to a percentage score, multiply it by 3.33.

Part 4: The writing tasks are evaluated holistically using scoring rubrics. The scale ranges from 0–5 and includes information from the reading and coherence/connectedness, paragraph development, structures and vocabulary from the unit, and errors.

Combining scores from Parts 1–3 and Part 4: To get a total Achievement Test score, multiply the writing test score by 2. Then, add the writing score to the score In Parts 1–3. Multiply this new score by 2.5 to get a percentage score.

Example 1	Example 2
Score on Test Parts 1–3 = 30	Score on Parts 1–3 = 23
Score on Part 4 = 5	Score on Part 4 = 3
Multiply 5 x 2	Multiply 3 x 2
Add 10 to 30	Add 6 to 23
Multiply 40 x 2.5	Multiply 29 by 2.5
Total score = 100%	Total score = 72.5%

Using the Scoring Rubrics

The *NorthStar Reading and Writing* rubrics are adapted from the integrated writing rubric of TOEFL iBT. Whereas the TOEFL iBT scoring rubric is intended to distinguish levels of English proficiency among candidates to colleges and universities, the *NorthStar* scoring rubrics are intended to show progress in students' writing at each of the five *NorthStar* levels. Therefore, *NorthStar* scoring bands make finer distinctions than TOEFL iBT's scoring band. In this way, students at each level will be able to both see improvement in their scores and receive high marks. The detailed scoring rubric is included in the Achievement Tests Answer Key.

Relationship between TOEFL iBT Rubric and *NorthStar 1* Integrated Writing Rubric		
TOEFL iBT		*NorthStar 1*
2–3		5
2		4
2		3
1–2		2
1		1
0		0

OTHER NORTHSTAR COMPONENTS

EXAMVIEW

NorthStar ExamView is a stand-alone CD-ROM that allows teachers to **create and customize** their own *NorthStar* tests.

DVD

The *NorthStar* DVD has **engaging, authentic video clips**, including animation, documentaries, interviews, and biographies, that correspond to the themes in *NorthStar*. Each theme contains a three- to five-minute segment that can be used with either the *Reading and Writing* strand or the *Listening and Speaking* strand. The video clips can also be viewed in MyNorthStarLab.

COMPANION WEBSITE

The companion website, www.longman.com/northstar, includes resources for teachers, such as the **scope and sequence, correlations** to other Longman products and to state standards, and **podcasts** from the *NorthStar* authors and series editors.

UNIT 1 The Friendship Page

OVERVIEW

Theme: Friendship

This unit explores forms of communication, the Internet, and the notion of friendship. Students evaluate different websites depending on how they are managed and developed and discuss the use of the Internet as a way for people to connect with others around the world. They also write a paragraph about a classmate and one of his or her friends.

Reading One: *Welcome to The Friendship Page* is an excerpt from a website written by its creator. She explains how she came to develop her website, who uses it, and how it functions.

Reading Two: *Welcome to MySpace* offers the description of the MySpace® site and its advantages and disadvantages.

Critical Thinking

Analyze a picture	Infer information not explicit in the text
Evaluate and compare Internet use	Hypothesize another's point of view
Analyze statistical information	Classify information
Infer word meaning from context	Support opinions with reasons

Reading

Predict content	Express opinions
Identify main ideas	Organize and synthesize information from the
Read for details	readings
Make inferences	

Writing

Write answers to questions	Order ideas
Use an interview as a pre-writing tool	Write a paragraph about a classmate
Construct complete sentences	

Vocabulary	Grammar
Use context clues to find meaning	Questions with *be* and *have*
Define words	
Use vocabulary for greetings	

📁 *MyNorthStarLab*	⚭ *Northstar: Listening and Speaking 1*
Readiness Check, Background and Vocabulary, Readings One and Two, Notetaking and Academic Skills Practice, Vocabulary and Grammar, Writing the Final Draft, Achievement Test	Unit 1 describes the Friendship Force, an international organization that promotes peace through homestays.

1

①FOCUS ON THE TOPIC

◀ SKILLS

Interpret a photograph; evaluate and compare Internet use; infer the meaning of new vocabulary from context.

✱✱✱Ⓐ PREDICT

Suggested Time: 10 minutes

1. Have students read the title of the unit, analyze the photo montage, and read the questions.

2. Discuss the questions as a class. Be sure students know the definition of *friendship*.

Expansion/Homework

For homework or language lab work, ask students to conduct a web search for social networking sites (key words: social networking sites). Ask students to choose one site they find and describe it to the class.

✱✱Ⓑ SHARE INFORMATION

Suggested Time: 20 minutes

1. Have students read the chart in **Exercise 1** individually. Check comprehension by asking the class questions such as: *What does it mean to download music? What travel plans can you make online? How many Americans use e-mail?*

2. Have students answer the questions in **Exercise 2**. Then divide the class into pairs and have each pair discuss the questions. Provide help with vocabulary where necessary.

Expansion/Homework

You may want to have students survey each other on how they use the Internet using the categories from the chart. The class can compile the information in a chart entitled *How People in Our Class Use the Internet*. Then students can compare their chart to the one in the book.

✦✦✦ C BACKGROUND AND VOCABULARY

📁 Go to www.mynorthstarlab.com for *Background and Vocabulary*.

Suggested Time: 20 minutes

1. Ask students to read the sentences, paying attention to the boldfaced words. Then, using context, have them choose the best definition for each boldfaced word. Move around the room and offer assistance if necessary.

2. Go over the answers as a class. Take the opportunity to show students how to use context clues in the sentences to understand the meaning of the vocabulary item. For example, for item 1 (*Bronwyn wants to help her **community** in Melbourne. She wants to help people in other countries, too.*), the word *too* indicates the second sentence is another example of something appearing earlier. *Wants to help* appears in both sentences. Students can deduce *community* and *people in other countries* are referring to each other. Then, looking at the examples, students can choose the best answer from the choices given. Also, students can replace the boldfaced word with the choices given; only one makes sense.

📁 Go to www.mynorthstarlab.com for additional *Background and Vocabulary* practice.

② FOCUS ON READING

◖ SKILLS

Predict the content of the reading; identify main ideas and details; make inferences based on the information in the reading; express opinions about The Friendship Page; read an excerpt from a website.

✦✦✦ A READING ONE: Welcome to The Friendship Page

📁 Go to www.mynorthstarlab.com to read and listen to *Welcome to The Friendship Page*.

Suggested Time: 20 minutes

Reading One is an excerpt from The Friendship Page website, in which its creator describes why she developed the website and the site's goals. She also writes about how the site is managed and who uses it. The style of the reading is informal.

1. Ask students to read the website title and the quote. Give them two minutes to check their predictions listed in **Exercise 1**.

2. Call on students to share their predictions with the class. Affirm each prediction as a possibility.

3. Have students read the text. The reading can be assigned as homework or lab work using MyNorthStarLab. You can also choose to play the recording of the reading and have students listen as they read.

4. For **Exercise 2**, have students turn to their predictions. Ask them if their predictions were confirmed by reading the text.

READING STRATEGY: Preparing to Read

1. Ask students to create a chart with headings labeled *What I Know*, *What I Expect to Learn*, and *What I Learned*.

2. Before reading, ask students to look at the title and accompanying picture. Determine what they already know about the topic by activating or creating background knowledge. Model filling in the first two columns on the board. Then have students complete the chart on their own. Accept all answers including what students know and what they think they know. The validity of the responses can be confirmed or denied after reading.

✪✪✪ READ FOR MAIN IDEAS   Suggested Time: 10 minutes

Have students complete the exercise individually. Go over the answers as a class. If there is any disagreement, ask students to point to the parts in the text that support the correct answers.

Expansion/Homework
This is a good opportunity to work with students on reading strategies. Most students have reading strategies they employ in their first language. Elicit a few strategies from students such as underlining and taking notes in the margins. Introduce some of your own as well.

✪✪✪ READ FOR DETAILS   Suggested Time: 15 minutes

1. Elicit the difference between main ideas and details. Explain that details support the main ideas of a text. For example, the two statements in the Read for Main Ideas section give very general information about The Friendship Page. The details give specific information such as dates and numbers.

2. If necessary, have students read the text again. Then divide the class into pairs (of mixed fluency if possible) and have students complete the sentences with the appropriate numbers. Have students underline the information as they find it in the text.

3. Go over the answers with the whole class. Ask individual students to read the details they completed. Ask students where the detail can be found in the text.

Expansion/Homework
The Reading for Main Ideas and/or Reading for Details exercises could be assigned for homework. The answers could then be discussed in class, first in pairs and then as a whole class.

✪✪✪ MAKE INFERENCES

1. Explain that in the following exercise, students must decide if the statement is true or false based on information from the text. Tell students that the answers are not directly in the text; they have to decide on the correct answers based on what they read and their opinions about it.

2. Divide the class into pairs. Have the pairs complete the activity. Have students point to the parts of the text that support their opinions.

3. Go over the answers as a class and explain the answers if necessary.

✪✪✪ EXPRESS OPINIONS

Suggested Time: 15 minutes

1. Tell students that it is now their turn to express their own opinions about the topic of The Friendship Page.

2. Have students complete the questions individually. Encourage them to check all answers that apply and add more of their own.

3. Call on a few students to share their answers with the class. Encourage them to support their answers with reasons.

Expansion/Homework

For homework, you may want to have students write short sentences giving examples or reasons for their answers.

CRITICAL THINKING

Have students read the following statements independently to judge whether each statement is true or false. If false, have students write a corrected statement. Next, students will work with a partner to share their initial responses and defend their answer choices. Return to a whole-class discussion to review.

1. Bronwyn Polson wanted to help her friend.

   Answer: False. Bronwyn Polson wanted to help her <u>community</u>.

2. You can get advice about friendship.

   Answer: True

3. The Friendship Page was started last year.

   Answer: False. The Friendship Page was started <u>in 1996</u>.

4. A goal of The Friendship Page is to make money.

   Answer: False. A goal of The Friendship Page is to <u>make the Internet friendlier</u> or <u>bring more peace to the world</u>.

5. Personal information is not allowed on this website.

   Answer: True

Link to *NorthStar: Listening and Speaking 1*

If students are also using the companion text, you might want to have them compare The Friendship Page with the Friendship Force. You can ask them: *Which organization is more interesting to you? Why?*

✪✪✪ B READING TWO: Welcome to MySpace

📁 Go to www.mynorthstarlab.com to read and listen to *Welcome to MySpace*.

Suggested Time: 15 minutes

Reading Two is a description of a popular social networking website called MySpace. Students read about the history of the site and how it operates. They also read about some problems associated with the site.

1. Explain that there are many other websites that meet various needs. Have students brainstorm what kinds of things people could have in common that they might like to share on a website (cooking, outdoor activities, restaurants, movies, etc.).

2. Ask students if they are familiar with or have visited MySpace. If so, have them explain what it is. If not, explain it is a website where many people enter information about themselves, describing their likes, dislikes, hobbies, families, etc. and share it with other people.

3. Have students read the text individually. Move around the classroom and help with any difficult vocabulary. You can also choose to play the recording of the reading and have students listen as they read.

4. Have students work individually and decide whether the statements are true or false. Then go over the answers as a class.

✪✪✪ C INTEGRATE READINGS ONE AND TWO

◖ **SKILLS**

Organize information from the readings in a chart; synthesize information from the readings to write answers.

STEP 1: Organize

1. Point to the chart and go through the points with the class.

2. Divide the class into pairs and have students complete the exercise.

3. Match two pairs of students and have them compare their answers.

4. Go over the answers with the entire class.

STEP 2: Synthesize

1. Explain that students are going to imagine they are Bronwyn Polson, the creator of The Friendship Page. Have each student write his or her responses to the questions. The responses do not need to be complete sentences.

2. Have students work in pairs. One student is Bronwyn Polson. The other student interviews her. When they are done, have the pairs switch roles. Move around the room and provide help where necessary.

3. When all students are finished, invite a few pairs to come up and act out their interviews.

   Go to www.mynorthstarlab.com for *Notetaking* and *Academic Skills Practice*.

③ FOCUS ON WRITING

Ⓐ VOCABULARY

◖ SKILLS

Review vocabulary from Readings One and Two; apply vocabulary learned in the unit to a new context—a passage on the creator of The Friendship Page; expand vocabulary by learning and practicing expressions for greetings and saying good-bye; use new vocabulary creatively by completing a conversation.

✪ REVIEW

   Go to www.mynorthstarlab.com for *Review*.

1. Have students read through the whole exercise before filling in the blanks. Then have them work individually to complete the exercise.

2. Call on individual students to say their answers. If there's disagreement, they should explain their answers.

1. Go over the explanation and expressions with the class.

2. Have students complete the exercise. Call on students to read their completed conversations. Correct if necessary.

3. As a follow-up, you may want to have students walk around the room, approach other students, and practice one of the conversations.

Expansion/Homework

Students should be encouraged to create lists of words and phrases they have learned. Encourage them to keep a separate notebook with phrases and vocabulary categorized by topic.

VOCABULARY EXPANSION: Word Relationships

1. This strategy may be used before reading to introduce vocabulary or after reading to reinforce the learning of the new words. Use the list of vocabulary from the text. You may wish to ask students to propose other unfamiliar words to make a list of 8–10 new words.

2. In small groups, students record one word with its definition on an index card. Each word should have its own card. Assign the task of grouping the vocabulary words based on how they are related to one another. Students may chose to group words alphabetically, by part of speech, or by definition. A representative from each group will explain the relationship of the words grouped together.

✪ CREATE

Suggested Time: 20 minutes

1. Ask if any students have screen names. Have students say their screen names. If they do not have one, have students create one. Ask a few students to share their screen names.

2. Ask if anyone has used chat rooms. If so, have a student describe what a chat room is. If not, tell the class that chat rooms are places people can talk online (in writing).

3. Explain to students that they will have a chat room conversation. Have students complete the conversation individually. Remind students to use the vocabulary from Review and Expand.

4. Have students practice their conversations with two other students.

5. Have a few students volunteer to read their conversations for the class.

Expansion/Homework

Ask students to contact a classmate on The Friendship Page in a chat room and have a conversation. They can arrange a date and time when they will both be online. Ask students to print the conversation or write it down. Have them bring it to class.

 Go to www.mynorthstarlab.com for additional *Vocabulary* practice.

B GRAMMAR: Questions with *Be* and *Have*

 Go to www.mynorthstarlab.com for *Grammar Chart* and *Exercise 3*.

◖ SKILLS

Form questions and answers with *be* and *have*.

Suggested Time: 25 minutes

1. Have pairs take turns reading the questions and answers in **Exercise 1**.

2. Have students complete **Exercise 2**. Call on students to read the underlined verbs and subjects. Correct if necessary.

3. Go over the charts with the class. Ask individual students to read the explanations and the examples. Point out that questions that begin with a form of *be* and *do* are answered *yes* or *no*.

4. Have students complete **Exercise 3** individually by writing out the questions. Next, have them exchange their questions with a partner and answer their partner's questions.

5. Go over the answers as a class. Correct if necessary.

Expansion/Homework
(1) Have students write a list of answers. Have them bring the lists to class and write them on the board. As a class, write the questions. (2) For further practice, offer exercises from *Focus on Grammar 1*, 2nd Edition or Azar's *Basic English Grammar*, 3rd Edition. See the Grammar Book References on page 225 of the student book for specific units and chapters.

Go to www.mynorthstarlab.com for additional *Grammar* practice.

C WRITING

If you wish to assign a different writing task than the one in this section, see page 24. The Alternative Writing Topics can also be assigned as additional writing topics for homework. The alternative topics relate to the theme of the unit, but they may not target the same grammar or rhetorical structures taught in the unit.

◖ SKILLS

Use an interview as a pre-writing tool; understand the components of a sentence; organize ideas into a paragraph; integrate the concepts, vocabulary, grammar, and rhetorical structures from the unit to write a paragraph about a classmate and one of his or her friends.

✪✪✪ PREPARE TO WRITE: Interviewing

Suggested Time: 20 minutes

1. Explain to students that as a culminating activity, they will write a paragraph about a classmate and one of his or her friends. Go over the information in the task box with the class.

2. Read the explanation with the class. Then have students choose one classmate to interview. Have them use the prompts to ask the questions. Encourage them to ask additional questions as well. Have students take turns interviewing each other, writing out answers in complete sentences. Walk around the classroom and provide assistance if necessary.

✪✪✪ WRITE: A Sentence

Suggested Time: 40 minutes

1. Go over the introduction and the information in the chart with the class. Offer additional examples if necessary. You might want to write additional sentences on the board and have students identify the parts.

2. Have students complete **Exercise 1**. Go over the answers with the class. If there is disagreement, have students explain their answers.

3. Have students complete **Exercise 2** individually. When they are done, have them compare their answers with another student's. If their answers are different, students should explain why. Go over the correct answers as a class.

4. With the same partners, have students complete **Exercise 3**. Go over the answers as a class.

5. Students are now ready to write their first drafts. Explain that the first draft is different from the final draft. The first draft is an opportunity for students to get their ideas on paper. They will have an opportunity to correct errors later. Have students choose one of the sentences in the box in **Exercise 4** to start their paragraphs. Move around the room and offer assistance if necessary. You may also want to assign writing the first draft for homework.

Expansion/Homework

If you assign writing the first draft for homework, students might want to use their computers to write their first drafts. Encourage students not to use computer tools such as spell check when working on their paragraphs. Be aware of unusual words or phrases that they may find through direct translation.

✪✪✪ REVISE: Ordering Your Ideas

Suggested Time: 20 minutes

1. Read the information about a paragraph with the class. Explain to students that a paragraph is a collection of sentences that deal with the same topic. Have students read the two paragraphs and write the number of sentences each paragraph has.

2. Read the information about paragraph organization with the class. Explain that writers might choose different ways to organize ideas. Emphasize that neither is better than the other, as long as the organization of the paragraph is clear.

3. Have students read the paragraphs in **Exercise 1** and **Exercise 2**. Then have them complete **Exercise 3**. Call on individual students to read their answers.

4. Read the instructions for **Exercise 4**. Have students return to their interviews and order their ideas. Move around the classroom and offer assistance as necessary.

✪✪✪ EDIT: Writing the Final Draft

Suggested Time: 20 minutes

Have students write the final drafts of their paragraphs. Encourage them to use language and grammar from the unit. Make sure they go through the checklist before submitting their final drafts. Collect the paragraphs and correct them before the next class.

Link to *NorthStar: Listening and Speaking 1*
If students are also using the companion text, you might want to have them write an expository paragraph about visiting and living in another culture.

 Go to www.mynorthstarlab.com for *Writing the Final Draft.*

✪ ALTERNATIVE WRITING TOPICS

These topics give students an alternative opportunity to explore and write about issues related to the unit theme.

✪ RESEARCH TOPICS

Suggested Time: 20–30 minutes in class

1. Have students turn to page 218. Review the instructions for the activity with the class. Make sure students understand the concept of a tribute.

2. Have students complete the task at home. In class, call on students to share their tributes with the class. If you have a large class, have students share their tributes in groups.

Go to www.mynorthstarlab.com for *Student Writing Models, Integrated Task, Video Activity, Internet Activity,* and *Unit 1 Achievement Test.*

What Will I Wear?

Theme: Fashion

This unit deals with the topic of school clothing. Students evaluate the appropriateness of various kinds of clothing for school, discuss whether students should be required to wear uniforms or not, and write a letter with an opinion describing a dress code they think is a good idea.

Reading One: *A Letter from the Principal* is a letter from a school principal announcing a new policy that all students must wear uniforms.

Reading Two: *School Newspaper Editorial* is a response to the new policy by a student.

Critical Thinking

Classify clothing	Infer information not explicit in the text
Rank the appropriateness of types of clothing	Support opinions with reasons
Interpret a graph	Determine a point of view
Infer word meaning from context	

Reading

Predict content	Express opinions
Identify main ideas	Organize and synthesize information from the
Read for details	readings
Make inferences	

Writing

Complete a role play	Brainstorm ideas for writing
Complete sentences	Order descriptive adjectives
Answer questions	Write an opinion letter

Vocabulary	Grammar
Use context clues to find meaning	The future with *will*
Define words	
Classify vocabulary	

MyNorthStarLab	*Northstar: Listening and Speaking 1*
Readiness Check, Background and Vocabulary, Readings One and Two, Notetaking and Academic Skills Practice, Vocabulary and Grammar, Writing the Final Draft, Achievement Test	Unit 2 focuses on the concept of recycling and reusing clothing in fashion and quilt making, and its benefits to the environment.

①FOCUS ON THE TOPIC

◖ SKILLS

Classify clothing; rank the appropriateness of types of clothing; interpret a graph; infer the meaning of new vocabulary from context.

✪✪✪Ⓐ PREDICT

Suggested Time: 15 minutes

1. Ask students if they have ever had to wear a school uniform. Pay special attention to defining the term *uniform*. Encourage them to discuss if they liked it or not and why.

2. See if students can identify which students in the pictures are wearing uniforms. Then have students label the clothing in pictures A and B.

3. Discuss question 3 as a class.

✪✪Ⓑ SHARE INFORMATION

Suggested Time: 15 minutes

1. Copy the graph from page 26 on the board. Use yourself as an example. Ask students if what you are wearing is OK for school. Encourage them to support their opinions with reasons. Give other examples of clothing and ask the class to respond if it is OK for school or not. Use the opportunity to define the words.

2. Divide the class into small groups of three or four students and have each group look at the four pictures and write the number they choose on the line. Tell them there is no correct answer. If there is disagreement, encourage students to discuss their opinions.

Expansion/Homework
To stimulate discussion, you could bring pictures of people in various outfits to use as examples.

📁 Go to www.mynorthstarlab.com for *Background and Vocabulary*.

Suggested Time: 25 minutes

1. Read the introductory paragraph aloud as students follow along. Discuss with students the difference between public and private schools.

2. Ask students to look at the graph in **Exercise 1**. Ask the class to identify the title of the graph. Point out the percentages on the left side, the responses along the bottom, and the percentages of responses. Have the class answer the question under the graph.

3. Take the opportunity to have students identify the source and year of the information. Ask students if they think the information in the graph is reliable and why.

4. Have students complete **Exercise 2**. Move around the room and explain unfamiliar vocabulary if necessary. Then go over the answers with the class.

5. Have students work in pairs and complete **Exercise 3**. Then call on pairs to read their answers to the class. Encourage discussion.

📁 Go to www.mynorthstarlab.com for additional *Background and Vocabulary* practice.

②FOCUS ON READING

◖ SKILLS

Predict the content of the reading; identify main ideas and details; make inferences based on the information in the reading; express opinions about reasons listed in the letter; read a newspaper editorial.

★★★ **A** READING ONE: A Letter from the Principal

📁 Go to www.mynorthstarlab.com to read and listen to *A Letter from the Principal*.

Suggested Time: 10 minutes

Reading One is a letter from a school principal to parents informing them about a new school policy requiring all students to wear uniforms. The letter identifies the policy and reasons for it.

1. Go over the instructions and the two sentences with the class. Then have students read the first sentence in the letter.

2. Have students check the sentence they think is true. Call on students and have them explain why they chose a particular sentence.

1. Direct instruction of vocabulary will aid students in learning difficult words that are not part of their daily experiences. Before reading, teach specific words from the text. Practice using the new words in different contexts. Provide repeated exposure to the newly learned words.

2. Read a sentence from the text that contains a target word. Ask students to use prior knowledge and context clues to determine the meaning of the word. Explain to students that context clues are like riddles. They provide help in determining the meaning of words. Point out helpful context clues in the reading. *They will think about school and schoolwork, not about* **fashion***. Today students think too much about clothes and how they look.* Cite other examples using definition, example, synonym, and antonym clues. Ask students, *Which word or words tell you what (target word) means?*

3. In addition to learning strategies, students may need to use a dictionary. Demonstrate how to find the word and discuss each definition to decide which best suits the context of the sentence. Continue to model this procedure until students are able to proceed alone or with a partner.

REACHING ALL STUDENTS: Reading Vocabulary

- **Less Proficient:** In addition to context clues, use role playing to provide verbal and visual cues to help determine the meaning of words.

- **More Proficient:** Have students use target vocabulary to write a business letter to inform.

✪✪✪ READ FOR MAIN IDEAS   **Suggested Time: 15 minutes**

1. Have students read the letter. The reading can be assigned as homework or lab work using MyNorthStarLab. You can also choose to play the recording of the reading and have students listen as they read.

2. Have students complete the exercise individually. Go over the answers as a class. If there is any disagreement, ask students to point to the parts in the text that support the correct answers.

✪✪✪ READ FOR DETAILS   **Suggested Time: 15 minutes**

1. Elicit the difference between main ideas and details. Explain that details support the main ideas of a text. For example, a detail might describe an object by identifying the color.

2. If necessary, have students read the letter again. Have students look back at their answer in Read for Main Ideas, then scan the letter for details that support the answers and underline them. Divide the class into pairs (of mixed fluency if possible) and have students compare the words they underlined.

3. Have students complete the exercise. Ask individual students to read the details they completed. Ask students where the detail can be found in the text.

Expansion/Homework
The Read for Main Ideas and/or Read for Details activities could be assigned for homework. The answers could then be discussed in class, first in pairs and then as a whole class.

✪✪✪ MAKE INFERENCES   Suggested Time: 10 minutes

1. Explain that in this exercise students will infer information from what they read; the answer is not a sentence in the text but rather something they must figure out based on what they read.

2. Have students work in pairs and complete the exercise. Then call on individual students to share their answers with the class. If there is disagreement, have students point to the information in the text that supports the correct answers.

✪✪✪ EXPRESS OPINIONS   Suggested Time: 15 minutes

1. Tell students that it is now their turn to express their own opinions about the reasons given for requiring school uniforms.

2. Have students work alone to complete the chart. You can do the first item as an example.

3. When students are done, have them work in pairs to compare their answers. Encourage students to explain their opinions.

Expansion/Homework
Students can be asked to think of more reasons for or against school uniforms. Discuss them at the beginning of class the next day.

CRITICAL THINKING

Give students the following questions for discussion in small groups before discussing as a whole class:

1. Who wrote the letter?

   Answer: Peter Collins, Principal of Lincoln High School

2. What is the purpose of this letter?

   Answer: The purpose of this letter is to inform students and parents about the school uniforms.

3. Name two reasons for having a school uniform.

   Answers will vary. Students can provide reasons from the letter or from their own experience.

✪✪✪ B READING TWO: School Newspaper Editorial

📁 Go to www.mynorthstarlab.com to read and listen to *School Newspaper Editorial*.

Suggested Time: 15 minutes

In Reading Two, students read an editorial column from the school newspaper in response to the principal's new policy. Students are given the opportunity to learn about the issue of school uniforms from a student's perspective and to familiarize themselves with a style of newspaper editorial.

1. Ask students if they have ever read a school newspaper. Ask them what kind of information is included in a school newspaper.

2. Explain that many people write to school as well as local newspapers when they want to comment on a recent article or event. Describe that an editorial is a newspaper or magazine article that gives the opinions of the editor or publisher. Tell them they are going to read an editorial from a school newspaper.

3. Have students read the text in **Exercise 1** individually. Move around the room and help with any difficult vocabulary. You can also choose to play the recording of the editorial and have students listen as they read.

4. Go over the comprehension questions in **Exercise 2** as a class. Ask students where in the letter the answers can be found.

Expansion/Homework
If your school has a school newspaper, you could bring it in and discuss what kinds of articles are in it. If there is an editorial section, discuss the kinds of topics discussed.

✪✪✪ C INTEGRATE READINGS ONE AND TWO

◖ SKILLS

Organize information from the readings in a chart; synthesize information from the readings to complete a conversation.

STEP 1: Organize

1. Tell students to return to Readings One and Two and think of arguments for and against school uniforms. Then elicit an example for each from the class.

2. Divide the class into pairs and have students complete the exercise. Then go over the answers with the class.

STEP 2: Synthesize

1. Explain that students are going to create a role play based on the information in the chart they completed in Step 1. Tell students that they should make the conversation as natural as possible.

2. Divide the class into pairs and have students complete the exercise. Move around the room and provide help where necessary.

3. When all students are finished, invite a few pairs to come up and act out their conversations for the class.

Go to www.mynorthstarlab.com for *Notetaking* and *Academic Skills Practice*.

③ FOCUS ON WRITING

Ⓐ VOCABULARY

◖ SKILLS

Review vocabulary from Readings One and Two; learn and practice expressions for getting dressed and wearing clothes; use new vocabulary creatively by describing pictures.

✪ REVIEW

Go to www.mynorthstarlab.com for *Review*.

1. Complete the first item with the class. Explain the words in bold are scrambled and students must put the letters in the correct order to spell a word. Point out that all words have been introduced previously in the unit. You can suggest two strategies students can use to unscramble the words—they can use context in each sentence, or they can look at the length of each word.

2. Have students complete the exercise. Then call on individual students to read their answers. Write the unscrambled words on the board. Read each word aloud and have students repeat chorally.

Expansion/Homework

Encourage students to write their own sentences using the vocabulary words, scrambling one word. Have students write their sentences on the board the next day. Use it as a warm-up activity to review the vocabulary from this unit.

Link to *Northstar: Listening and Speaking 1*

If students are also using the companion text, you might want to create similar exercise using vocabulary from the *Listening and Speaking* strand.

✪✪ EXPAND   Suggested Time: 15 minutes

1. Read the sentences in the chart as a class. Point to the pictures to illustrate the meaning of the boldfaced words. Ask individual students to make their own sentences using the word or phrase.

2. Have students work individually to complete their own sentences. Then have students compare their complete sentences with a partner's.

3. Call on individual students to come to the board and write their sentences.

VOCABULARY EXPANSION: Contractions

1. Provide a list of contractions for students to record. (For example, *she'd* = *she* + *would*.)

   aren't = _____ + _____   it's = _____ + _____   she's = _____ + _____

   can't = _____ + _____   here's = _____ + _____   they'll = _____ + _____

   it'll = _____ + _____   there's = _____ + _____   we're = _____ + _____

2. Ask students to work in groups to fill in the blanks. Have students pronounce each contraction and provide the two words used to form it.

3. To practice using the words, provide each student with an index card and assign either a contraction or two words. Collect the cards and shuffle before redistributing. Students conceal the card and walk around the room greeting each other and asking, *What card do you have?* When a match is made, students may be seated.

✪ CREATE   Suggested Time: 15 minutes

1. Explain to students that they will write sentences about the man in the pictures. As a warm up, have students suggest a few sentences aloud.

2. Have students work individually to write five sentences about the pictures. Encourage them to use as many vocabulary words as possible.

3. Call on individual students to write sentences on the board. If there are errors, encourage the class to correct them.

Expansion/Homework

Ask students to find a find a photograph of a person from the Internet, a book, or a magazine. Have students write a short paragraph about the person using as much target vocabulary from the unit as possible. Have all students tape the pictures to the board and then take turns reading the paragraph aloud, not identifying which picture they are describing. Other students can guess which picture is being described.

 Go to www.mynorthstarlab.com for additional *Vocabulary* practice.

B GRAMMAR: The Future with *Will*

 Go to www.mynorthstarlab.com for *Grammar Chart* and *Exercise 2*.

◖ SKILLS

Learn to use *will* to talk about the future in questions and sentences.

Suggested Time: 20 minutes

1. Have students complete **Exercise 1** by going back to Reading Two and identifying sentences that use *will*. Have students write the sentences on the lines. Explain that we use *will* to talk about the future.

2. Ask a few students what they will do tonight and tomorrow. Elicit responses and write them on the board, correcting for grammar. Ask students to identify which word shows the event will occur in the future. Underline *will*. Point out that the verb that follows *will* is in base form.

3. Go over the information in the chart with the class. Offer additional explanations and examples if necessary.

4. Have students complete **Exercise 2**. Call on individual students to read their answers to the class. Encourage other students to correct any errors.

Expansion/Homework
For further practice, offer exercises from *Focus on Grammar 1*, 2nd Edition or Azar's *Basic English Grammar*, 3rd Edition. See the Grammar Book References on page 225 of the student book for specific units and chapters.

 Go to www.mynorthstarlab.com for additional *Grammar* practice.

C WRITING

If you wish to assign a different writing task than the one in this section, see page 42. The Alternative Writing Topics can also be assigned as additional writing topics for homework. The alternative topics relate to the theme of the unit, but they may not target the same grammar or rhetorical structures taught in the unit.

Use brainstorming as a pre-writing tool; use descriptive adjectives; give reasons with *because*; integrate the concepts, vocabulary, grammar, and rhetorical structures from the unit to write an opinion letter.

✪✪✪ PREPARE TO WRITE: Brainstorming

Suggested Time: 15 minutes

1. Explain to students that as a culminating activity, they will write an opinion letter addressing a dress code and why they think it is a good idea. Go over the information in the task box with the class.

2. Explain that to begin, students need to generate ideas. One way to generate ideas is to brainstorm. The goal is to make a list of ideas, so any idea is fine. Students should not stop to think, but just write whatever comes to mind. Once students are done brainstorming, they will choose the best idea to write about.

3. Have students write their ideas on a separate piece of paper so they are not limited by space. Have them complete items 1–3.

4. When they are done, ask students to share their ideas with the class.

✪✪✪ WRITE: A Letter with an Opinion

Suggested Time: 40 minutes

1. Ask students if they can remember writing an opinion letter in their native language. Ask for examples. Elicit the contents of an opinion letter and write them on the board. (For example, your opinion of the problem, ideas to address the problem, why your solution is good)

2. Write two sentences on the board: one that is a statement and one that is an opinion using *I think that*. Ask students to identify the difference. Explain that *I think that* is a way to express an opinion. Point out the difference between formal writing and everyday speaking.

3. Have students work in pairs and complete **Exercise 1**. When done, ask the class the questions and let students volunteer responses. Write some of the responses on the board.

4. Have students complete **Exercise 2** individually. Ask for volunteers to write answers on the board.

5. Using the sentences on the board, add a reason to your opinion statement using *because*. Explain that when you give an opinion, you often give a reason for your opinion.

6. Complete the first item in **Exercise 3** with the class. Encourage students to come up with reasons, and emphasize that there is no right or wrong opinion.

7. Have students complete the exercise. Call on individual students to read their sentences to the class. Correct any errors.

8. Explain that students will now write their own letter. Have students complete **Exercise 4** individually. Remind them to answer the questions about the place they will write about in their letters. Once students complete Exercise 4, have them complete the letter in **Exercise 5**. Move around the room and offer assistance if necessary. You can also assign writing the first draft for homework.

✪✪✪ REVISE: The Order of Descriptive Adjectives

Suggested Time: 20 minutes

1. Ask students to describe your clothes. They will likely start with the names of the items (pants, shirt). Ask them follow-up questions such as color, pattern, or material. Generate as much vocabulary as possible.

2. Write a sentence on the board using students' responses about your clothing and following the order of the chart on page 41. If one detail is missing, leave a space. Go back and ask a question to generate a response. Then label each adjective following the chart on page 41.

3. Explain that descriptive adjectives add details to "make a picture." The adjectives follow an order in a sentence and come before the noun.

4. Have students complete tasks 1 and 2. Ask for volunteers to read their sentences to the class. Encourage the class to correct ordering if necessary.

5. Have students complete task 3. Tell them to underline adjectives in their letter and find places where they could add more adjectives.

Expansion/Homework
Have students add one or two words to each column in the chart on page 41.

✪✪✪ EDIT: Writing the Final Draft

Suggested Time: 20 minutes

Have students write the final drafts of their letters. Encourage them to use language and grammar from the unit. Make sure they go through the checklist before submitting their final drafts. Collect the letters and correct them before the next class.

Link to *NorthStar: Listening and Speaking 1*
If students are also using the companion text, have them write an opinion letter about the benefits of using recycled materials in fashion design.

 Go to www.mynorthstarlab.com for *Writing the Final Draft*.

✪ ALTERNATIVE WRITING TOPICS

These topics give students an alternative opportunity to explore and write about issues related to the unit theme.

✪ RESEARCH TOPICS

Suggested Time: 20–30 minutes in class

1. Have students turn to pages 218–219. Review the instructions for the activity with the class. Help students identify people that they can interview.

2. Have students complete the research and prepare a short presentation.

3. Have students share their research findings with the class or in small groups.

 Go to www.mynorthstarlab.com for *Student Writing Models, Integrated Task, Video Activity, Internet Activity,* and *Unit 2 Achievement Test.*

OVERVIEW

Theme: The arts

This unit explores the life and work of Keith Haring. Students evaluate various pieces of art and discuss what constitutes a piece of art and what the boundaries of art are. They also write a short biography of Keith Haring.

Reading One: *Art for Everyone* is a magazine interview, in which *Art World Magazine* interviews Edwin T. Ramoran from the Bronx Museum of the Arts about Keith Haring's life and art.

Reading Two: *Look at Haring's Art* is a descriptive paragraph about two of Keith Haring's pieces.

Critical Thinking

Analyze a picture

Interpret paintings

Infer word meaning from context

Infer information not explicit in the text

Categorize information

Reading

Predict content

Identify main ideas

Read for details

Make inferences

Read a timeline

Correct false statements

Express opinions

Organize and synthesize information from the readings

Writing

Complete sentences

Complete a crossword puzzle

Find information in the reading

Give events in time order

Use commas in dates and names of places

Write a biography

Vocabulary

Use context clues to find meaning

Define words

Classify vocabulary by part of speech

Grammar

Simple past of *be* and *have*

📁 *MyNorthStarLab*
Readiness Check, Background and Vocabulary, Readings One and Two, Notetaking and Academic Skills Practice, Vocabulary and Grammar, Writing the Final Draft, Achievement Test

👓 *Northstar: Listening and Speaking 1*
Unit 3 focuses on the topic of rap music.

FOCUS ON THE TOPIC

◖ SKILLS

Analyze a photograph; interpret and discuss paintings; infer the meaning of new vocabulary from context.

✪✪✪Ⓐ PREDICT

Suggested Time: 10 minutes

1. Have students look at the picture and discuss the questions as a class.

2. Ask students if they think it is OK to draw on the subway walls. Why would someone draw in a public place?

3. Ask students what they think "art" is or is not.

Expansion/Homework

Ask students if they have a favorite artist. Have students bring in an image by the artist and share it with the class. Students can tell the class what they know of the artist and his or her work.

✪✪Ⓑ SHARE INFORMATION

Suggested Time: 15 minutes

1. Draw students' attention to the pictures. Have a general discussion about the pictures, eliciting what students see, what they think it means, why someone would draw or paint these images.

2. Divide the class into pairs and have each pair discuss the questions in the chart. Move around the classroom and provide help with vocabulary where necessary.

3. Ask for pairs to share their responses.

✪✪✪Ⓒ BACKGROUND AND VOCABULARY

 Go to www.mynorthstarlab.com for *Background and Vocabulary*.

Suggested Time: 20 minutes

1. Ask students to read the vocabulary words and definitions in **Exercise 1**. If students are having difficulty with certain words, provide sample sentences.

Elicit sample sentences from students as well. Correct for grammar when repeating students' sentences.

2. Go over pronunciation of words as a class.

3. Have students complete **Exercise 2** and then go over the answers as a class.

Expansion/Homework

For homework, have students write a short description of their favorite picture or painting using as many of the target words as possible.

Go to www.mynorthstarlab.com for additional *Background and Vocabulary* practice.

FOCUS ON READING

◖ SKILLS

Read a timeline; categorize information; identify main ideas; read for details; make inferences based on the information in the reading; express opinions about Keith Haring's art; read a descriptive paragraph.

 **READING ONE: Art for Everyone**

Go to www.mynorthstarlab.com to read and listen to *Art for Everyone*.

Suggested Time: 20 minutes

Reading One is a magazine interview in which students read about the life and work of Keith Haring. The style of the interview is somewhat informal.

1. Explain to students that a timeline is a way to visually show events in order. Have them look at the timeline in **Exercise 1**. To familiarize them with the structure of a timeline, ask students to identify events in Keith Haring's life such as when he was born or when he died.

2. Have students read the timeline individually. When they are done, review the information by asking them questions about some of the events (for example, *When was he arrested for drawing in the subway?*).

3. Have students complete the chart in pairs. Go over the answers as a class. If there is any disagreement, ask students to point to the appropriate information in the timeline that supports their answers.

4. Finally, have students read the interview in **Exercise 2**. The reading can be assigned as homework or lab work using MyNorthStarLab. You can also choose to play the recording of the reading and have students listen as they read.

1. As a whole class, look at the title and format of the selection to predict what the text is about. Use these ideas to activate prior knowledge of the content and organizational style. Ask students to provide other examples of non-fiction texts, specifically interviews.

2. Write a list of the following words from the selection: *paintings, Keith Haring, social issues, famous, graffiti, museums, New York.* Allow time for individuals to think independently about the words.

3. In small groups, have students make predictions or ask questions about the text. Following the reading, students return to their groups to check predictions and answer pending questions.

✪✪✪ READ FOR MAIN IDEAS   Suggested Time: 10 minutes

Have students complete the exercise individually. Go over the answers as a class. If there is any disagreement, ask students to point to the information in the text that supports the correct answers.

✪✪✪ READ FOR DETAILS   Suggested Time: 15 minutes

1. If necessary, have students read the interview again. Then divide the class into pairs (of mixed fluency if possible) and have students complete the sentences. Encourage them to underline the information in the interview that supports the correct answers.

2. Call on individual students to read the answers to the class.

Expansion/Homework
Have students cover the vocabulary choices for Read for Details and see if they can fill in the words on their own.

✪✪✪ MAKE INFERENCES   Suggested Time: 10 minutes

1. Explain to students that inferencing is important to understanding the meaning of certain information that is not said in a text, but can be guessed from what is said. Explain that based on the information in the interview, many people liked Keith Haring's work. The interview doesn't say "people liked his work," but students can infer or understand it from reading the whole interview.

2. Explain that in the following exercise students must infer why people liked Keith Haring's work.

3. Have students work with a partner to complete the exercise. Then go over the answers as a class. Encourage discussion if there is disagreement. Encourage students to offer their own ideas as well.

1. Tell students that it is now their turn to express their own opinions about the topic of Keith Haring's art.

2. Have students work in small groups and discuss the two sentences. This will help them generate ideas. After a short discussion, students can individually write their own sentences.

3. Ask for volunteers to share their sentences with the class. Emphasize that there is no right or wrong answer. Students can agree and add an idea of their own.

Expansion/Homework

For homework, you can have students write a short paragraph giving their opinions on Keith Haring's art.

CRITICAL THINKING

Give students the following questions for discussion in small groups before discussing as a whole class:

1. What was the relationship between Edwin Ramoran and Keith Haring?

   Answer: Ramoran worked in an art museum and Haring was an artist.

2. What are the three kinds of Haring's art that people started to buy?

   Answer: drawings, paintings, sculptures

3. What is public art?

   Answer: Art painted in public places like in subways and on walls of buildings

4. Keith Haring first became famous for his public art. Some people say it is just graffiti. Do you support this kind of art?

   Answers will vary, but students should support their opinions with convincing reasons.

5. In your own words, describe Keith Haring.

   Answers will vary, but they should be supported by the text.

REACHING ALL STUDENTS: Critical Thinking

- **Less Proficient:** Accept one-word simple phrase answers. Check frequently for understanding and provide specific feedback.

- **More Proficient:** Have students visit www.haring.com for additional information about the artist and add details to their answers.

READING TWO: Look at Haring's Art

📁 Go to www.mynorthstarlab.com to read and listen to *Look at Haring's Art.*

Suggested Time: 10 minutes

In Reading Two, students read a descriptive paragraph about two pieces of Keith Haring's art. The reading gives students the opportunity to learn more about Haring's art and the social and political issues that were important to Haring.

1. Ask students if they ever go to museums to look at art. If so, ask what they look for in art (color, line, shapes, message, etc.). If not, ask them why they think people do like to look at art. Also encourage discussion about why people create art.

2. Draw students' attention to the two pictures on page 51. Ask what they think the pictures represent.

3. Have students read the paragraph in **Exercise 1** individually. You can also choose to play the recording of the paragraph and have students listen as they read. Then have them complete **Exercise 2**.

4. Have students compare their answers with another student's. Have students identify where in the text they found the answers.

5. Go over the answers as a class.

✿✿✿ C **INTEGRATE READINGS ONE AND TWO**

◖ **SKILLS**

Organize information from the readings in a chart; synthesize information from the readings to complete sentences.

STEP 1: Organize   **Suggested Time: 15 minutes**

1. Review all of Keith Haring's pictures in the unit. Review the names of each piece and discuss what important ideas each represents.

2. Have students complete the exercise and then compare their answers with a partner's.

3. Go over the answers with the entire class. Encourage discussion.

STEP 2: Synthesize   **Suggested Time: 15 minutes**

1. Go over the instructions for the activity with the class. Then have students complete the sentences.

2. When students are done, have volunteers read the answers.

Link to *Northstar: Listening and Speaking 1*

If students are also using the companion text, ask them to compare rap to Keith Haring's work. Ask them: *What are your opinions about rap? Does it have a political message? If so, what is it? Is it effective?*

Go to www.mynorthstarlab.com for *Notetaking* and *Academic Skills Practice*.

3 FOCUS ON WRITING

A VOCABULARY

◖ SKILLS

Review vocabulary from Readings One and Two; apply vocabulary learned in the unit to a new context—a crossword puzzle; identify and analyze word forms; use new vocabulary creatively by writing sentences about Keith Haring and his art.

✪ REVIEW   Suggested Time: 15 minutes

1. Go over the crossword puzzle with the class.

2. Have students work in pairs to complete the puzzle.

3. Have pairs work with another pair to compare answers.

Link to *NorthStar: Listening and Speaking 1*

If students are also using the companion text, have pairs create crossword puzzles using the vocabulary from Unit 3 of the *Listening and Speaking* strand.

✪✪ EXPAND   Suggested Time: 20 minutes

Go to www.mynorthstarlab.com for *Expand*.

1. Go over the three parts of speech with the class. Ask students if they can define what a noun, adjective, and verb are. Explain to students that some words can function as more than one part of speech.

2. Go over the chart in **Exercise 1**. Elicit sample sentences using the words in the chart.

3. Go over the definitions and examples on page 55.

4. Have students complete **Exercise 2**.

5. Call on individual students to read their completed sentences to the class.

Expansion/Homework

(1) Exercise 2 can also be assigned for homework. (2) For homework, you might want to give students a list of words from the previous units and have them categorize the words in a chart similar to the chart on page 54.

 Link to *NorthStar: Listening and Speaking 1*

If students are also using the companion text, have them categorize the words from Unit 3 of the *Listening and Speaking* strand in a chart similar to the chart on page 54.

VOCABULARY EXPANSION: Linking Unknown Words to Existing Knowledge

1. Review the list with students to select unknown words. Then model the following think-aloud process for linking an unknown word to existing knowledge: *The word "graffiti" is defined as "words written on public sidewalks or walls." I have seen words, but also pictures painted in public spaces. For example, there are gang signs spray-painted on the stop sign near my house. I have also heard of people creating art on the walls of train stations in other cities. Some people like this type of artwork, but others do not think public space is the appropriate place for it.*

2. Ask for student volunteers to explain another word from the group's vocabulary list. Remind them to state the word, define the word, and offer examples. Following a whole group discussion of the word list, students create their own relationships and include an illustration.

✪ CREATE

Suggested Time: 15 minutes

1. Explain to students that they will write sentences about Keith Haring. Tell them they can use the words from the chart on page 54.

2. Have students write their sentences individually and then exchange papers with a partner who will check the sentences for errors.

3. Call on individual students to read their sentences to the class.

Expansion/Homework

Ask students to write three sentences about another artist they know. Let students read their sentences to the class. Encourage them to bring in a sample of the artist's work.

Go to www.mynorthstarlab.com for additional *Vocabulary* practice.

Go to www.mynorthstarlab.com for *Grammar Chart* and *Exercise 2*.

◖ **SKILLS**

Learn the simple past of *be* and *have* and write questions and answers.

Suggested Time: 30 minutes

1. Have students read the excerpt from the interview in **Exercise 1** and underline *was, were,* and *had*. Then have them write the number of times they saw the words. Call on individual students to share their answers with the class.

2. Go over the information in the charts. Be sure to point out third-person singular and plural of *be*. Compare *yes/no* and *wh-* questions with *be*. For *have*, emphasize the difference between affirmative and negative (*had, did not have*) and between *yes/no* questions and *wh-* questions (*did* + base form).

3. Have students complete **Exercise 2** individually. When done, have students switch papers with another student to correct. If there is disagreement, students should use the charts to explain. Then go over the answers as a class.

4. Have students complete **Exercise 3** individually. Then have students exchange their books with a partner and complete **Exercise 4** by answering each other's questions. When done, have students switch the books again. Call on individual students to read their questions and their partner's answers.

Expansion/Homework

For further practice, offer exercises from *Focus on Grammar 1*, 2nd Edition or Azar's *Basic English Grammar*, 3rd Edition. See the Grammar Book References on page 225 of the student book for specific units and chapters.

 Go to www.mynorthstarlab.com for additional *Grammar* practice.

C **WRITING**

If you wish to assign a different writing task than the one in this section, see page 64. The Alternative Writing Topics can also be assigned as additional writing topics for homework. The alternative topics relate to the theme of the unit, but they may not target the same grammar or rhetorical structures taught in the unit.

◖ **SKILLS**

Find relevant information in the reading; order events chronologically; use commas in dates and the names of places; integrate the concepts, vocabulary, grammar, and rhetorical structures from the unit to write a biography of Keith Haring.

✪✪✪ PREPARE TO WRITE: Finding Information in a Reading

Suggested Time: 15 minutes

1. Explain to students that as a culminating activity, they will write a biography of Keith Haring. Go over the information in the task box with the class.

2. Ask students if they have ever read a biography in their native language. Ask what kind of information is included in a biography. Make a list on the board (for example, dates, places, family information, education, work, interests, major events).

3. Explain to students that in order to write a biography of Keith Haring, they need information about Keith Haring's life. Explain that they will get that information from the timeline and Reading One.

4. Have students work alone to complete **Exercise 1**. Encourage students to write complete sentences. Then have them share their answers with a partner.

5. Have students complete **Exercise 2** and write the additional information on the line.

6. Have the class share other ideas they want to include in their biography.

✪✪✪ WRITE: Time Order

Suggested Time: 40 minutes

1. Ask students who have read biographies to describe the order in which the information is usually presented. If students have not read biographies, ask what order they think would be best.

2. Have students work alone to complete **Exercise 1**. Then have them compare their answers with another student's (**Exercise 2**). If there are differences, have students discuss and come to an agreement. Go over the answers as a class.

3. Read the instruction for **Exercise 3** and have students order the answers to the questions from Exercise 1 in Prepare to Write.

4. Ask students what a good topic sentence would be. Write some examples on the board. Discuss why the examples are good or what needs to be added (Do they clearly explain what the paragraph will be about? Are they too general or too specific?).

5. Read the instructions for **Exercise 4** with the class. Have students write their topic sentences, then add the other sentences that support the main idea. Emphasize that this is the first draft. Students should not be worrying about grammar, spelling, or punctuation, just ideas. Students can also complete their first drafts for homework.

✪✪✪ REVISE: Using Commas in Dates and the Names of Places

Suggested Time: 20 minutes

1. Go over the examples in **Exercise 1**. Describe where the commas go. Compare examples such as *May 4, 1958* versus *in May of 1958*. Ask students to notice the difference (one is a complete date). Compare other examples to generate rules (*from Kutztown* versus *from Kutztown, Pennsylvania*).

2. Go over the rules for comma use with the class.

3. Have students complete **Exercise 2**. Have them identify which punctuation rule applies to each item in Exercise 2. You might want to assign numbers to the rules to help with the discussion. Go over the answers as a class.

4. Have students individually complete **Exercise 3**. Ask for volunteers to write sentences on the board. Correct errors as a class.

✪✪✪ EDIT: Writing the Final Draft

Suggested Time: 20 minutes

Have students write the final drafts of their biographies. Encourage them to use language and grammar from the unit. Make sure they go through the checklist before submitting their final drafts. Collect the biographies and correct them before the next class.

Link to *NorthStar: Listening and Speaking 1*
If students are also using the companion text, you might want to have them write a history of rap music.

Go to www.mynorthstarlab.com for *Writing the Final Draft.*

✪ ALTERNATIVE WRITING TOPICS

These topics give students an alternative opportunity to explore and write about issues related to the unit theme.

✪ RESEARCH TOPICS

Suggested Time: 20–30 minutes in class

1. Have students turn to page 219. Review the instructions for the activity with the class.

2. Have students complete the research about the artist they have chosen and write a paragraph answering the questions.

3. In class, have students exchange their paragraphs and pictures with a partner and answer the questions. Call on individual students to share what they have found out.

 Go to www.mynorthstarlab.com for *Student Writing Models, Integrated Task, Video Activity, Internet Activity*, and *Unit 3 Achievement Test.*

What's It Worth to You?

OVERVIEW

Theme: Special possessions

This unit focuses on the theme of antique collecting. Students explore and discuss the topic of collecting valuable or special possessions. They also write a descriptive paragraph about a special possession or collection.

Reading One: *My Secret* is a sports column, in which the author, a sports journalist, confesses to being a fan of the television show *Antiques Roadshow*.

Reading Two: *Be a Smart Collector* is a list of rules for anyone interested in becoming a collector.

Critical Thinking

Interpret an illustration

Discuss possessions

Infer word meaning from context

Support opinions with reasons

Infer information not explicit in the text

Categorize information

Relate information in the unit to personal experiences

Reading

Predict content

Identify main ideas

Read for details

Make inferences

Match examples to information in the reading

Express opinions

Organize and synthesize information from the readings

Writing

Complete a short paragraph

Ask questions

Stay on topic

Write a paragraph about a special possession or collection

Vocabulary	Grammar
Use context clues to find meaning Define words Find word association Classify vocabulary	The simple present

MyNorthStarLab
Readiness Check, Background and Vocabulary, Readings One and Two, Notetaking and Academic Skills Practice, Vocabulary and Grammar, Writing the Final Draft, Achievement Test

Northstar: Listening and Speaking 1
Unit 4 deals with jewelry, especially the value of diamonds and their social significance.

① FOCUS ON THE TOPIC

(SKILLS

Interpret an illustration; discuss possessions; infer the meaning of new vocabulary from context.

✿✿✿ A PREDICT

Suggested Time: 10 minutes

1. See if students can guess who the people are (buyer, seller, collector, owner of the watch, friends). Ask what the significance of the date (1932) could be, who the old man is, and why he is giving the watch to the younger man.

2. Ask students if they have ever been given something valuable that is old or if they have any valuable family objects that have been passed down.

3. Discuss the questions as a class. Elicit responses from students and write them on the board.

✿✿ B SHARE INFORMATION

Suggested Time: 20 minutes

1. Discuss the idea of collecting things (stamps, coins, dolls). Ask why people collect things (for enjoyment, value, hobby, tradition). Ask students if any of them are collectors, or if any of their friends or family members are collectors, and what they collect.

2. Have students write their special possession in the chart. If they don't have one, they can write the name of a family member or friend who collects or has a special possession. Then have students mingle and complete the chart. For students who finish ahead of others, have them interview one or two more students.

Expansion/Homework
For homework, have students write a paragraph about one of the people they interviewed. Have them describe the person's valuable possession or collection and the reasons for having it. Have students share their paragraphs in small groups.

📁 Go to www.mynorthstarlab.com for *Background and Vocabulary*.

Suggested Time: 20 minutes

1. Explain that students will read a passage with boldfaced words. The boldfaced words are vocabulary items. They should pay special attention to the words because they will have to match them to the definition later. This is using context clues to guess meaning.

2. Have students read the passage.

3. Have students work in pairs to match the boldfaced words with their definitions.

4. Go over the answers with the class. Give examples of using context if necessary, for example, "People can *learn* a lot on this show. It is very **educational**." Explain that often words are defined in the sentence that follows or precedes the sentence with the word in question.

📁 Go to www.mynorthstarlab.com for additional *Background and Vocabulary* practice.

②FOCUS ON READING

◖SKILLS

Predict reasons; identify main ideas; read for details; make inferences; express opinions about a TV show; read a list.

📁 Go to www.mynorthstarlab.com to read and listen to *My Secret*.

Suggested Time: 20 minutes

Reading One is a sports column, in which the author, a sports journalist, describes his secret of being a fan of the TV show *Antiques Roadshow.* He explains how he hopes the show comes to his town so he can take his special possession, a baseball signed by Babe Ruth. The style is somewhat informal.

1. Ask students to read the beginning of the column in **Exercise 1**. Ask what they think Dan Stone's secret is. Affirm each prediction as a possibility.

2. Have students read the article in **Exercise 2**. Ask if their predictions were confirmed by reading the text. The reading can be assigned as homework or lab work using MyNorthStarLab. You can also choose to play the recording of the reading and have students listen as they read.

READING STRATEGY: Interacting with Text

1. Model fluent reading to demonstrate the ability to read text accurately and quickly. Reread the selection, stopping at critical points to think aloud. Demonstrate interacting with the text by asking yourself questions such as: *What is happening? What will happen next? What in the text helped make that prediction?*

2. Have students work with a partner to read the text and form questions to guide their reading. Student A will begin reading. At the end of the first paragraph, the reader will stop and ask the listener: *What is happening? What do you think will happen next? What in the text helped you make that prediction?* Monitor students' progress.

✪✪✪ READ FOR MAIN IDEAS   Suggested Time: 10 minutes

Have students complete the exercise individually. Go over the answers as a class. If there is any disagreement, ask students to point to the parts in the text that support the correct answers.

Expansion/Homework
(1) You can assign the reading and the exercise as homework. Students can then compare their answers in class. (2) Students may write their own true/false statements about the article. In groups, students can read their statements, decide if they are true or false, and locate where they found the answer in the text.

✪✪✪ READ FOR DETAILS   Suggested Time: 15 minutes

1. If necessary, have students read the article again. Then have them complete the exercise. Then go over the answers with the whole class.

2. Reiterate how details support main ideas. Ask what main idea each detail supports. For example, the fact that friends think Dan Stone watches something on Monday night is a main idea. What he watches (*Antiques Roadshow*) is a detail.

REACHING ALL STUDENTS: Reading for Details

| • **Less Proficient:** Work with students in a small group to provide repeated practice interacting with text. | • **More Proficient:** Have students record their thoughts as they read. |

✪✪✪ MAKE INFERENCES   Suggested Time: 10 minutes

Have students work individually to complete the exercise. As they finish, pair them up to discuss their answers. If there is disagreement among students, welcome it. Encourage them to support their answers with information from the reading.

1. Tell students that it is now their turn to express their own opinions about *Antiques Roadshow*.

2. Ask students if they would watch *Antiques Roadshow* and ask them to explain their reasons. Ask if they have any items they would like to take on the show.

3. Have students work in groups of three to complete the activity. Encourage students to support their answers with information from the reading.

4. Call on individual students to share their answers with the class. Encourage discussion if there is disagreement.

Expansion/Homework

(**1**) Students can have a debate on the value of educational shows like *Antiques Roadshow* versus shows for entertainment only. If you choose to do this activity, let students get in two groups and brainstorm ideas for their side. Then explain that one side is to give a reason and support it. The other side then gives a reason and supports it. (**2**) This can also be done as a writing activity. The reasons serve as the main ideas. The support is the detail.

CRITICAL THINKING

Give students the following questions for discussion in small groups before discussing as a whole class:

1. What is the writer's favorite TV show?

   Answer: The writer's favorite TV show is *Antiques Roadshow*.

2. What adjectives does the author use to describe the TV show *Antiques Roadshow?*

   Answer: *Antiques Roadshow* is exciting, educational, and simple.

3. What happens on the show after the guests tell the experts about their items?

   Answer: After the guests tell the experts about their items, the experts talk about the items and assess their value.

4. Based on the text, how can you tell that *Antiques Roadshow* is a popular TV show?

   Answer: The author says that 14 million people watch the show every week.

5. Would you sell a valuable antique if it had sentimental value?

   Answer: Answers will vary, but students should support their responses with clear reasons and examples.

READING TWO: Be a Smart Collector

📁 Go to www.mynorthstarlab.com to read and listen to *Be a Smart Collector*.

Suggested Time: 15 minutes

In Reading Two, students read a list of tips for becoming a successful collector. The goal of the reading is to deepen students' knowledge of the art of collecting by reading tips written by an expert.

1. Ask students again about collecting. If they are collectors, ask them what they collect and what advice they would give for becoming a good collector. If they are not collectors, ask if they have any interest in collecting and what they would collect if they could start today. Ask what questions they would want to ask an expert to get started collecting.

2. Have students read the text in **Exercise 1** individually. Move around the room and help with any difficult vocabulary. You can also choose to play the recording of the reading and have students listen as they read.

3. Have students complete **Exercise 2**. Then go over the answers as a class. Ask students what language in the rule made them choose their answer.

★★★ **C** **INTEGRATE READINGS ONE AND TWO**

◀ **SKILLS**

Organize information from the readings in a chart; synthesize information from the readings to complete a short paragraph.

STEP 1: Organize   **Suggested Time: 15 minutes**

1. Read the instructions with the class. Point to the chart and explain the rules are on the left. Students are to find information in the first reading that goes with each rule.

2. Have students complete the exercise. Then go over the answers with the class. Encourage discussion if there is disagreement.

STEP 2: Synthesize   **Suggested Time: 15 minutes**

1. Tell students that they are going to explain if Dan Stone is or is not a smart collector based on the information in the chart they completed in Step 1.

2. Have students start by having a discussion to decide if Dan Stone is or isn't a smart collector and then list reasons to support their decision. Then have them write 4–5 sentences explaining their opinion. Move around the room and provide help where necessary.

3. When all students are finished, invite a few volunteers to read their sentences.

Link to *NorthStar: Listening and Speaking 1*

If students are also using the companion text, you might want to have them read the movie review of *Blood Diamond* on page 73. Discuss the impact a valuable item can have on people. Who do you think should keep the diamond and why?

Go to www.mynorthstarlab.com for *Notetaking* and *Academic Skills Practice*.

③ FOCUS ON WRITING

Ⓐ VOCABULARY

◖ SKILLS

Review vocabulary from Readings One and Two; expand vocabulary by identifying word forms; use new vocabulary creatively by writing sentences about special possessions.

✪ REVIEW   Suggested Time: 10 minutes

Go to www.mynorthstarlab.com for *Review*.

1. Have students complete the exercise. Move around the room and offer assistance if necessary.

2. Have students compare their answers in pairs. Then go over the answers as a class.

Expansion/Homework
For homework, you can have students write their own sentences with the words in parentheses.

✪✪ EXPAND   Suggested Time: 15 minutes

1. Write *noun, adjective,* and *verb* on the board, leaving space between and below. Review the definitions and the word endings. Get examples of each type and write them on the board below each category.

2. Have students complete the exercise with a partner. While students are working, copy the chart on the board.

3. Ask individual students to come to the board and write the words in the correct column.

Link to *NorthStar: Listening and Speaking 1*
If students are also using the companion text, you might want to have them group the vocabulary from Unit 4 of the *Listening and Speaking* strand.

VOCABULARY EXPANSION: Vocabulary Games

1. Divide students into groups of four. Each team will define several words from the list.

antiques	exciting	history	sentimental
collection	experts	million	valuable
condition	favorite	rare	worth
educational	guests	secret	

Each member of the group is charged with one of the following tasks: (1) scramble the letters so that the word is not easily apparent; (2) define the word; (3) identify the part of speech; (4) locate and write the sentence in the text containing the target word.

2. Next, each group presents the word group assigned. Have them begin by asking others to unscramble and identify the word by spelling it correctly and then proceed with the other information. Finally, classmates propose a simple visual that would best represent the new word. The group selects one visual symbol. These may be used to play a game similar to *Pictionary*. One student will draw the symbol and others guess the word. They may also be required to provide the spelling, definition, and part of speech.

✪ CREATE
Suggested Time: 15 minutes

1. Explain to students that they will write sentences about a special possession. Tell them that if they do not have one, they can write about an imaginary possession.

2. Have students write their sentences individually and then exchange papers with a partner who will check the sentences for errors.

3. Call on individual students to read their sentences to the class.

 Go to www.mynorthstarlab.com for additional *Vocabulary* practice.

✪✪ B GRAMMAR: The Simple Present

Go to www.mynorthstarlab.com for *Grammar Chart* and *Exercise 2*.

◖ SKILLS

Learn to use the simple present in sentences, *yes/no* questions, and *wh-* questions.

Suggested Time: 25 minutes

1. Read the excerpt with students. Then have them complete **Exercise 1** individually. Go over the answers as a class.

2. Go over the chart with the class. Ask individual students to read the explanations and the examples. Have students add their own examples.

3. Point out the use of *do* and *does*. Ask a few questions of the class. Let volunteers answer.

4. Have students complete **Exercise 2** individually, then compare their answers with a partner's.

5. To check answers, have two students read the conversation aloud to the class. Correct errors.

Expansion/Homework

(**1**) Ask students to have the same conversation as a role play. You can either have them write it out, focusing more on accuracy, or have them act it out, focusing more on fluency. (**2**) For further practice, offer exercises from *Focus on Grammar 1*, 2nd Edition or Azar's *Basic English Grammar*, 3rd Edition. See the Grammar Book References on page 225 of the student book for specific units and chapters.

 Go to www.mynorthstarlab.com for additional *Grammar* practice.

C WRITING

If you wish to assign a different writing task than the one in this section, see page 81. The Alternative Writing Topics can also be assigned as additional writing topics for homework. The alternative topics relate to the theme of the unit, but they may not target the same grammar or rhetorical structures taught in the unit.

(SKILLS

Ask questions; understand the components of a paragraph; identify topic sentences; stay on topic; integrate the concepts, vocabulary, grammar, and rhetorical structures from the unit to write a paragraph about a special possession.

✪✪✪ PREPARE TO WRITE: Questioning Yourself

Suggested Time: 20 minutes

1. Explain to students that as a culminating activity, they will write a paragraph about a special possession. Go over the information in the task box with the class.

2. Explain to students that one way to get ideas is to ask questions. In this activity, they will question themselves on a special possession.

3. Have students work individually to complete **Exercises 1** and **2**. Encourage them to think of anything they consider special; it does not need to be special to anyone else. They should feel free to choose any item.

4. Then match two pairs and have students share their lists and their answers to the questions. Invite any volunteers to share with the rest of the class.

5. For **Exercise 3**, have students choose one possession to write about.

✪✪✪ WRITE: A Paragraph

Suggested Time: 45 minutes

1. Go over the explanation of the structure of a paragraph with the class. Answer questions and offer additional information if necessary.

2. Have students read the sample paragraph in **Exercise 1** and answer the questions. Go over the answers as a class.

3. Have students complete **Exercise 2**. Emphasize that the sentences are already in the correct order. Students are focusing on the structure of a paragraph. Move around the room and offer assistance where necessary.

4. Have students read the paragraph in **Exercise 3** and identify the topic sentence. Go over the answer with the class.

5. Have students read the paragraph in **Exercise 4** and identify the best topic sentence. Go over the correct topic sentence, pointing out why it is the best and why the others are not correct. (Answer **b** is correct because it is about the shirt and why it is important, which is the topic.)

6. Go over the instructions for **Exercise 5**. Move around the room and help students write their topic sentences. It is important that everyone have a good topic sentence to work from.

7. Have a few students write their topic sentences on the board. Discuss them: Are they describing a main idea? Are they general enough? Discuss what details the students could include in their paragraphs.

8. Go over the instructions for **Exercise 6** and then have students write the first drafts of their paragraphs. Don't allow students to use a dictionary while writing as this will slow down the process. The core vocabulary they need is all available in the unit. Remind students to include detail sentences. Emphasize that they will worry about grammar later; this is the time to focus on ideas. You can also assign writing the first draft for homework.

✪✪✪ REVISE: Staying on the Topic

Suggested Time: 20 minutes

1. Reinforce that the topic sentence gives the main idea of the paragraph, and all other sentences support the topic sentence. Any sentence about another topic does not belong in the paragraph.

2. Read the example paragraph as a class. Ask for a volunteer to read it aloud, or let several students take turns reading each sentence. Have students read all sentences, including the crossed-out sentence. When done, discuss the topic, and point out that the topic sentence is underlined. Ask why the one sentence is crossed out (it's about another topic). Go over each of the other sentences in the paragraph and show how they are related to the topic.

3. Have students individually read the paragraph in **Exercise 1**, underline the topic sentence, and cross out any sentences that do not belong. Then have students work with a partner to compare answers. If there is disagreement, students should explain their choices. Then go over the answers as a class.

4. Read the instructions for **Exercise 2** with the class. Have students look at their drafts, cross out any sentences that do not belong, and add any new sentences if necessary.

✪✪✪ EDIT: Writing the Final Draft

Suggested Time: 20 minutes

Have students write the final drafts of their paragraphs. Encourage them to use language and grammar from the unit. Make sure they go through the checklist before submitting their final drafts. Collect the paragraphs and correct them before the next class.

 Go to www.mynorthstarlab.com for *Writing the Final Draft.*

✪ ALTERNATIVE WRITING TOPICS

These topics give students an alternative opportunity to explore and write about issues related to the unit theme.

✪ RESEARCH TOPICS

Suggested Time: 20–30 minutes in class

1. Have students turn to page 220. Review the instructions for the activity with the class. Help students identify places they can visit and research.

2. Have students conduct the research and write the paragraph at home.

3. In class, have students exchange their paragraphs and photographs with a partner, read each other's paragraphs, answer the questions, and offer feedback.

 Go to www.mynorthstarlab.com for *Student Writing Models, Integrated Task, Video Activity, Internet Activity,* and *Unit 4 Achievement Test.*

UNIT 5
Strength in Numbers

OVERVIEW

Theme: Strength in numbers

This unit focuses on the social issues that affect young people and the programs that address these issues. Students learn about the Guardian and Urban Angels and how they help at-risk youths. Students explore the topic of how a group of people working together can make a difference for a community. They also write a letter to the editor describing a community program they support.

Reading One: *Urban Angels* is a brochure, in which frequently asked questions explain the work of the Guardian Angels.

Reading Two: *Two Real Angels* introduces two youths who are active in the Urban Angels program.

Critical Thinking

Analyze a picture

Rate social issues in your hometown

Infer word meaning from context

Infer information not explicit in the text

Support opinions with reasons

Categorize information

Reading

Predict content

Identify main ideas

Read for details

Make inferences

Express opinions

Read a chart

Organize and synthesize information from the readings

Writing

Complete sentences

Complete a letter

Make a list

Give examples to support opinions

Write a letter to the editor

Vocabulary

Use context clues to find meaning

Define words

Use idiomatic expressions

Grammar

Pronouns and possessive adjectives

MyNorthStarLab
Readiness Check, Background and Vocabulary, Readings One and Two, Notetaking and Academic Skills Practice, Vocabulary and Grammar, Writing the Final Draft, Achievement Test

Northstar: Listening and Speaking 1
Unit 5 deals with Alzheimer's disease, its effect on people who suffer from it and their families, and the benefits of support groups.

①FOCUS ON THE TOPIC

◖ SKILLS

Analyze a picture; interpret the title and content of the unit; rate social issues in your hometown; infer the meaning of new vocabulary from context.

✪✪✪ A PREDICT

Suggested Time: 10 minutes

1. See if students can identify where the group is (a large city).

2. Discuss the questions as a class. Pay special attention to defining the term *guardian*.

✪✪ B SHARE INFORMATION

Suggested Time: 15 minutes

1. Ask students to think of social problems that exist in large cities. Explain that social problems can include things that make life difficult. Discuss why social problems might exist (lack of jobs, education, housing) and what can be done to ease the problems (better schools, after-school programs, more jobs, better health care).

2. Divide the class into small groups of three or four students and have each group discuss the questions. Move around the room and ask questions. Provide help with vocabulary as necessary.

3. Discuss the answers as a class. Emphasize that there is no right or wrong answer. The answers are based on students' perceptions.

4. For students who are primarily from other locations, have a discussion about social problems that exist in their hometowns and if they differ from where they now live.

Expansion/Homework

To stimulate discussion, you could bring in a local newspaper and go over the headlines. Many may be difficult for students to understand, but you can have a general discussion on the types of problems reported in the news, both locally and worldwide.

📁 Go to www.mynorthstarlab.com for *Background and Vocabulary*.

Suggested Time: 20 minutes

1. Write the term *Guardian Angel* on the board. Help students understand the meaning of the two terms, and what they mean together. Explain that the picture on page 83 shows a group of people called Guardian Angels. Tell students they will read an excerpt from a website about the Guardian Angels

2. Have students read the text in **Exercise 1** individually, then work in a group of three to complete **Exercise 2**. Encourage students to point out the place in the text that helps them understand the meaning of the word.

3. Go over the answers as a class, using the text to help clarify meaning.

Expansion/Homework

To help students use context to understand the meaning of words, show them a few strategies. Some strategies are: *Is it a good or bad thing?* For example, *Some **at-risk** teenagers need help to stay out of trouble.* To understand **at-risk** teenagers, they look at *stay out of trouble* and understand that whatever *at-risk* means, it has to do with the possibility of being in trouble. Then show them how to look over the list of definitions to narrow down what it must mean. Other strategies include: *Is it the same or different? Is it an example of? Is it an adjective, noun, verb?*

📁 Go to www.mynorthstarlab.com for additional *Background and Vocabulary* practice.

②FOCUS ON READING

◖ SKILLS

Read a chart; interpret statistical information; rank problems; identify main ideas; read for details; make inferences; express opinions about a youth program; read a brochure.

📁 Go to www.mynorthstarlab.com to read and listen to *Urban Angels*.

Suggested Time: 20 minutes

Reading One is an informational brochure that explains the work and goals of the Urban Angels, a program run by the Guardian Angels. Urban Angels work to help at-risk teens stay in school and avoid trouble. The style is somewhat formal.

1. Have students study the chart in **Exercise 1**. Check understanding by having them identify the title, the time span (per month), and what is being reported.

Then have students list the problems from the most common to the least common. Call on individual students to read their lists to the class. If there is any disagreement, ask students to point to the appropriate information in the chart.

2. Write *Frequently Asked Questions/FAQ* on the board. Ask if students have ever seen either and if anyone knows what they mean. If not, explain that often people ask similar questions about a topic, so an organization or individual will write up the answers to the most commonly asked questions and make them available on the Internet or in a brochure for everyone to read.

3. Have students read the brochure in **Exercise 2**. Move around the room and help with vocabulary if necessary. The reading can be assigned as homework or lab work using MyNorthStarLab. You can also choose to play the recording of the reading and have students listen as they read.

READING STRATEGY: Graphic Organizers

1. In pairs, students will monitor their comprehension through the use of graphic organizers. A simple two-column organizer is created by folding paper in half lengthwise. Later, the organizer may be used as a study guide.

2. Assist students in creating a graphic organizer to guide their reading. Use the headings to develop questions to answer as they read each section. Explain to students that these questions help set a purpose for reading and will aid in focusing on the text. Write the questions on the left side of the page, allowing room for the answers to be written on the right side of the page. Student pairs read the text section by section and complete the chart. Encourage students to refer back to the text to develop their answers more fully. Monitor student responses to ensure comprehension.

REACHING ALL STUDENTS: Reading One

- **Less Proficient:** Have students work with small chunks of written material. Provide questions to serve as a guide where necessary.

- **More Proficient:** As they read, have students write questions and answers in complete sentences using correct spelling and punctuation.

✪✪✪ READ FOR MAIN IDEAS   Suggested Time: 10 minutes

Have students complete the activity individually. Go over the answers as a class. If there is any disagreement, ask students to point to the information in the text that supports the correct answers.

Expansion/Homework
(1) You can assign the reading and the exercise as homework. Students can then compare their answers in class. (2) You might want to have students rewrite false statements to make them true.

✪✪✪ READ FOR DETAILS

1. If necessary, have students read the brochure again. Then have students complete the exercise. Then go over the answers with the whole class. Alternatively, you can have students cover the right-hand column and then scan the text for the answers and write them out.

2. Ask individual students to read the details they completed. If time allows, ask students where the detail can be found in the text.

✪✪✪ MAKE INFERENCES

1. Remind students that inferences are guesses about the information in the text. Based on what they read, students will need to decide which information in the exercise they should check.

2. Have students complete the exercise and compare their answers with a partner's.

3. Go over the answers with the class. Encourage students to point to the places in the reading that support the answers.

✪✪✪ EXPRESS OPINIONS

1. Ask if anyone would like to be an Urban Angel. Why? What challenges do they think they would face? What would be the best and worst part of the job?

2. Tell students that it is now their turn to express their own opinions about the topic of Urban Angels and social problems in their city.

3. Have students complete the statement and discuss their answers with a partner.

4. Call on individual students to share their answers with the class. Encourage discussion.

Expansion/Homework
Students can be asked to write a short paragraph using their responses.

CRITICAL THINKING

Give students the following questions for discussion in small groups before discussing as a whole class:

1. What is the main idea of Paragraph 9?

   Answer: The main idea is to explain why Urban Angels have nicknames.

2. What is the name of the Urban Angels program?

   Answer: The name of the program is Life Skills Program.

(continued on next page)

3. Can anyone become an Urban Angel? Explain your answer.

Answer: No. You can become an Urban Angel if you are a teenager from the South Bronx or Washington, D.C.

4. List the ways in which the program helps teenagers. In your opinion, which of these is most important? Rewrite the list in the order of importance.

Answer: It helps teens avoid drugs, gangs, guns, crime, and other trouble; stay in school; and become positive members of society; it provides educational activities and special classes.

✪✪✪ B READING TWO: Two Real Angels

 Go to www.mynorthstarlab.com to read and listen to *Two Real Angels*.

Suggested Time: 15 minutes

Reading Two introduces two teens, Kathy and Melissa, who are active in their Urban Angels program. The purpose of the reading is to give students the opportunity to expand their knowledge of the Urban Angels and to learn about real people involved in the program.

1. Ask students why they think people like to be Urban Angels. What is the benefit of becoming an Urban Angel? Write some responses on the board.

2. Tell students they will read about two real Urban Angels.

3. Have students read the text in **Exercise 1** individually. Move around the room and help with any difficult vocabulary. You can also choose to play the recording of the reading and have students listen as they read.

4. Have students complete **Exercise 2**. Call on individual students to read their answers. If there is disagreement, ask students to point out the places in the text that support the correct answers.

✪✪✪ C INTEGRATE READINGS ONE AND TWO

◀ SKILLS

Organize information from the readings in a chart; synthesize information from the readings to complete a letter.

STEP 1: Organize   Suggested Time: 10 minutes

1. Review the main information about Urban Angels—who they are and what they do.

2. Explain that now students will determine which example from Reading One applies to which of the two Urban Angels they read about in Reading Two.

3. Have students complete the exercise.

4. While students are working, draw the chart on the board, leaving room for students to fill in answers.

5. Have several different students each write one example in the chart. Encourage discussion if there is disagreement.

STEP 2: Synthesize   **Suggested Time: 15 minutes**

1. Explain to students that they will need to use the information from the chart in Step 1 to complete a letter.

2. Have students complete the exercise. More around the room and offer assistance if necessary.

3. Call on individual students to read their letters to the class.

Link to *NorthStar: Listening and Speaking 1*

If students are also using the companion text, you might want to have them write a similar letter from a member of the writing group for Alzheimer's patients.

Go to www.mynorthstarlab.com for *Notetaking* and *Academic Skills Practice*.

③ FOCUS ON WRITING

Ⓐ VOCABULARY

◖ SKILLS

Review vocabulary from Readings One and Two; apply vocabulary learned in the unit to a new context—a description of a Canadian youth program; expand vocabulary by learning and using idiomatic expressions; use new vocabulary creatively by writing a letter.

✜ REVIEW   **Suggested Time: 15 minutes**

Go to www.mynorthstarlab.com for *Review*.

1. Draw students' attention to the picture on page 93. Have them look at the symbols and guess what they represent (art, dance, music, theater). Have students look at the name of the organization and then what the acronym stands for. Discuss "discipline" as it relates to art (studying, commitment, etc).

2. Tell students that they will read about another program for kids called DARE. Ask students to guess why the program might exist (to give kids something to do and keep them out of trouble).

3. Go over the first paragraph with the class, completing the missing word. Then have students complete the remaining paragraphs.

4. Ask for volunteers to read and supply missing words. Encourage students to read one sentence each so more students get to participate.

✪✪ EXPAND

1. Explain that idioms are expressions whose meanings are not always clear from understanding the individual words. Students usually have to memorize them. However, sometimes a visual can help.

2. Go over the idioms in **Exercise 1** with the class. Give visual explanations if helpful. Or, after explaining, ask students if they have a good visual.

3. Have students complete **Exercise 2** individually. Go over the answers with the class.

4. Have pairs practice the conversations. If time allows, call on pairs to read the conversations to the class.

Expansion/Homework
Students should be encouraged to keep a list of idioms they are learning. They can create flash cards with the idiom on the front and the definition and sample sentence on the back, keep an alphabetized list, or create a list by category ("food" idioms, "body parts" idioms, etc.).

VOCABULARY EXPANSION: Personal Associations

1. Ask students to choose 8–10 unknown or unfamiliar words from the readings. For each word, students should record the sentence from the text that contains the target word. They should write any other sentence(s) that gives a clue to its meaning.

2. Assign students the task of writing their own sentences using the vocabulary words. Encourage students to make a personal association with the word in their sentences. Challenge them to use two or more words in the same sentence.

✪ CREATE

1. Explain to students that they will write a letter about teenagers in their city.

2. Have students get into groups of four to five and brainstorm ideas. First, brainstorm problems teenagers in their city have (for example, they don't go to school, are part of gangs, do drugs, etc.), then brainstorm what the teenagers who don't have problems do (they go to school, they have jobs, etc.).

3. Ask for ideas from the groups and write them on the board in two columns. This will help those students who had trouble generating ideas.

4. Go over the parts of a letter (date, opening, body, closing, signature).

5. Have students write their letters individually. Encourage them to use the words from Review and Expand.

6. Call on individual students to read their letters to the class.

Expansion/Homework
You can assign the letter for homework after doing brainstorming in class.

 Go to www.mynorthstarlab.com for additional *Vocabulary* practice.

B GRAMMAR: Pronouns and Possessive Adjectives

 Go to www.mynorthstarlab.com for *Grammar Chart* and *Exercise 2*.

◀ SKILLS

Learn and practice using pronouns and possessive adjectives.

Suggested Time: 30 minutes

1. Write two sample sentences on the board, one using a noun subject, the next one using the appropriate pronoun in place of the noun. For example: *Carol is sitting by the door. She is reading an interesting book.* Write two other sample sentences, one using a noun object, the other a pronoum. For example, *Urban Angels help the youth in their neighborhood. Urban Angels help them stay out of trouble.* Write a few more pairs to get more examples. Ask students to identify what the pronoun is replacing (the noun subject or the noun object). Underline the noun and pronoun.

2. Explain that the words that replace the nouns are pronouns. Some pronouns replace subjects and some replace objects.

3. Have students complete **Exercise 1**. Call on individual students to answer the questions.

4. Go over the chart with the class. Ask individual students to read the explanations and the examples.

5. Have students complete **Exercise 2**. Go over the answers by calling on students to read their completed sentences. Have students explain why their answers are correct.

6. Have students complete **Exercise 3**. Call on individual students to read their completed paragraphs to the class.

Expansion/Homework
(1) You can assign Exercises 2 and 3 as homework and check answers in class.
(2) For further practice, offer exercises from *Focus on Grammar 1*, 2nd Edition or Azar's *Basic English Grammar*, 3rd Edition. See the Grammar Book References on page 225 of the student book for specific units and chapters.

 Go to www.mynorthstarlab.com for additional *Grammar* practice.

If you wish to assign a different writing task than the one in this section, see page 105. The Alternative Writing Topics can also be assigned as additional writing topics for homework. The alternative topics relate to the theme of the unit, but they may not target the same grammar or rhetorical structures taught in the unit.

◖ SKILLS

Organize ideas for writing; use examples; integrate the concepts, vocabulary, grammar, and rhetorical structures from the unit to write a letter to the editor about a community program.

✪✪✪ PREPARE TO WRITE: Making a List

Suggested Time: 20 minutes

1. Explain to students that as a culminating activity, they will write a letter to the editor of a local newspaper, in which they will explain why they support a group that helps their community. Go over the information in the task box with the class.

2. Explain to students that making a list is a good pre-writing activity to help get and organize ideas. In a list, the sentences do not need to be complete.

3. Start with a class discussion about local organizations that help the community. You might want to bring in a local paper that has ads for organizations and agencies. Discuss whom the organizations help (teens, kids, families, animals, homeless people, etc.). Next, discuss what kinds of things the organizations do (after-school programs, help with school work, health organizations, art, science, sports, etc.) and what types of activities might be involved (classes, workshops, field trips, activities, games).

4. Copy the chart from **Exercise 1** on the board and call on students to fill in the information.

5. Have students individually choose one organization they want to write about. Using the example in **Exercise 2**, have them make a list of the ways the organization helps.

6. Ask for volunteers to read their lists. Encourage students to suggest more ideas.

Link to NorthStar: Listening and Speaking 1
If students are also using the companion text, you might want to include the writing group for Alzheimer's patients in your discussion.

✪✪✪ WRITE: A Letter to the Editor

Suggested Time: 40 minutes

1. Ask students if they can remember reading or writing a letter to the editor in their native language. Elicit the structure of a letter to the editor and write the

key components on the board. If not, ask why someone would want to write a letter to the editor, then brainstorm the parts of a letter. Go over the information on page 100.

2. Read the sample letter to the editor in **Exercise 1** as a class. Go over the questions and answers. Have students find the information in the text and underline it.

3. Have students read the letter to the editor in **Exercise 2** and answer the questions. Go over the answers as a class.

4. Have students complete **Exercise 3**. Move around the room and offer assistance if necessary.

5. Go over the instructions for **Exercise 4**. Have students write their first drafts. Move around the room to help students with formulating the topic sentence and supporting details. You can also assign writing the first draft for homework.

Expansion/Homework
Bring in a local or school newspaper and show students examples of letters to the editor. Have students analyze the letters for structure and information that is included in the letter.

Link to NorthStar: Listening and Speaking 1
If students are also using the companion text, they can choose to write about support groups through the Alzheimer's Organization.

✪✪✪ REVISE: Introducing Examples

Suggested Time: 20 minutes

1. Go over the information about examples on page 103. Explain that in good writing, it is important to give an example of an idea. Examples are information that supports an opinion. Two ways to do that are to use the phrases *such as* and *for example*.

2. Have students complete **Exercise 1**. Call on individual students to share their answers with the class.

3. Go over the examples in **Exercise 2** and then have students complete the task. Go over the answers as a class.

✪✪✪ EDIT: Writing the Final Draft

Suggested Time: 20 minutes

Have students write the final drafts of their letters. Encourage them to use language and grammar from the unit. Make sure they go through the checklist before submitting their final drafts. Collect the letters and correct them before the next class.

 Go to www.mynorthstarlab.com for *Writing the Final Draft.*

✪ ALTERNATIVE WRITING TOPICS

These topics give students an alternative opportunity to explore and write about issues related to the unit theme.

✪ RESEARCH TOPICS

Suggested Time: 20–30 minutes in class

1. Have students turn to page 220. Review the instructions for the activity with the class. Tell students to use a search engine such as Google to find websites for organizations that help teenagers.

2. Have students design and write the advertisement for the Urban Angels at home. Encourage students to use photos, illustrations, or cartoons to make their advertisement interesting.

3. In class, have students display and present their advertisements. Have the whole class vote on the best and most effective advertisement.

Go to www.mynorthstarlab.com for *Student Writing Models, Integrated Task, Video Activity, Internet Activity*, and *Unit 5 Achievement Test.*

Going Out of Business?

Theme: Business

This unit explores the rise of chain stores, the demise of locally owned businesses, and the impact this change has on communities. Students focus on the topic of competition between small and large businesses and how small companies cannot compete with large companies. They also write a descriptive paragraph about a favorite place.

Reading One: *The Death of the Family-Owned Video Store?* is a newsletter article describing the effect large chain stores are having on small family-owned businesses.

Reading Two: *About BLOCKBUSTER Total Access™* is a webpage about Blockbuster's online access to its services.

Critical Thinking

Analyze a picture
Activate prior knowledge
Categorize stores in your neighborhood
Infer word meaning from context

Support opinions with reasons
Analyze an advertisement
Infer information not explicit in the text
Identify advantages and disadvantages

Reading

Read an advertisement
Predict content
Identify main ideas
Read for details

Make inferences
Express opinions
Organize and synthesize information from the readings

Writing

Write questions and answers
Write a descriptive paragraph about a business
Draw a map

Use space order
Write a paragraph about a place

Vocabulary	Grammar
Define words	*There is / There are*
Use context clues to find meaning	
Classify vocabulary	

📁 **MyNorthStarLab**
Readiness Check, Background and Vocabulary, Readings One and Two, Notetaking and Academic Skills Practice, Vocabulary and Grammar, Writing the Final Draft, Achievement Test

🔗 **Northstar: Listening and Speaking 1**
Unit 6 focuses on creativity in business by looking at a young company owner who developed a product and what business schools can learn from her.

1 FOCUS ON THE TOPIC

◖ SKILLS

Analyze a picture; activate prior knowledge; categorize stores in your neighborhood; infer the meaning of new vocabulary from context.

✸✸✸ Ⓐ PREDICT

Suggested Time: 10 minutes

1. Ask students to look at the picture and identify the two stores they see. Compare and contrast the stores (both sell coffee, one is large, one is small, one is open, one is closed).

2. Discuss the questions as a class. Then have students predict what the unit will be about. Affirm each prediction as a possibility.

Expansion/Homework
Have students look around their neighborhood for stores that might compete with each other because they sell the same products. Have students notice the size, location, and atmosphere of the stores. Have students compare the stores and predict what will happen to them. Will they both survive? Why or why not?

✸✸ Ⓑ SHARE INFORMATION

Suggested Time: 20 minutes

1. Read the paragraph on chain stores with the class. Discuss the meaning of *chain store*. Give several examples (Starbucks, Barnes and Noble, etc.). Discuss the difference between chain stores and local stores.

2. Have students work in groups of three or four and complete **Exercise 1**.

3. Go over the list as a class. Write the information on the board.

4. In the same groups, have students complete **Exercise 2**.

5. When done, have each group report on one chain store and one locally owned store and give reasons why they go or don't go to that store.

Expansion/Homework
(**1**) As a follow-up discussion, you could ask: *Are chain stores good for the community? Are locally owned stores good for the community? Why or why not?* (**2**) If students come from other countries or regions, they could describe which type of store (chain or locally owned) prevails in their home communities and why.

If students are also using the companion text, you might want them to discuss the following questions: *Do chain stores or locally owned stores sell more interesting and creative products?* Ask students to give examples.

✸✸✸ C   BACKGROUND AND VOCABULARY

📁 Go to www.mynorthstarlab.com for *Background and Vocabulary*.

Suggested Time: 25 minutes

1. Have students complete **Exercises 1** and **2** individually. Then call on students to read the answers to the class.

2. Have students read the ad in **Exercise 3**. Review the information in the ad by asking what the store provides and what students know about the prices, service, and selection.

3. Have students complete **Exercise 4**. Go over the answers as a class.

Expansion/Homework

To help students learn the vocabulary, have them work in pairs to quiz each other on the definitions. For example: *What can I get at a barbershop? You can get a haircut.* Have students switch roles so both get to ask and answer questions.

📁 Go to www.mynorthstarlab.com for additional *Background and Vocabulary* practice.

② FOCUS ON READING

◖ SKILLS

Predict content; identify main ideas; read for details; make inferences; express opinions about the future of the video store; read an excerpt from a website.

✸✸✸ A   READING ONE: The Death of the Family-Owned Video Store?

📁 Go to www.mynorthstarlab.com to read and listen to *The Death of the Family-Owned Video Store?*

Suggested Time: 20 minutes

Reading One is a newsletter article written by a local business owner who asks his customers to patronize locally owned businesses. Students also read about the problems caused by chain stores and specifically how large video stores could put a local video store out of business. The style is somewhat informal.

1. Ask students if they are familiar with Blockbuster. If not, explain that Blockbuster is a chain video store. Ask students how Captain Video and

Blockbuster might be the same or different. Ask how Captain Video's owner might feel if Blockbuster opened up in his town.

2. Have students read the short introductory paragraph and complete **Exercise 1**.

3. Call on students to read the words they think will appear in the newsletter. Affirm each word as a possibility. Then have students read the newsletter in **Exercise 2**. Encourage students to underline any words they do not know but to keep reading if they encounter an unfamiliar word. The reading can be assigned as homework or lab work using MyNorthStarLab. You can also choose to play the recording of the reading and have students listen as they read.

READING STRATEGY: Think-Pair-Share

After examining the title and previewing the text, read the passage aloud, stopping after each paragraph. The following questions model the type of inquiry to pose to student pairs. Students should take time to think independently about the question, pair with a partner, and share their ideas. Accept comments from the whole group before beginning the next paragraph.

Paragraph 1—What is the problem stated in the first paragraph?
Paragraph 2—What is the name of the video store?
Paragraph 3—Where is Captain Video located?
Paragraph 4—How many benefits does Captain Video offer?
Paragraph 5—How does Captain Video plan to keep a good movie selection?
Paragraph 6—What kind of service is provided?
Paragraph 7—Would you buy from Blockbuster or Captain Video?
Paragraph 8—What is the purpose of Paragraph 8?
Paragraph 9—What is the selection mostly about?

✪✪✪ READ FOR MAIN IDEAS   Suggested Time: 10 minutes

Have students complete the exercise individually. Go over the answers as a class. If there is any disagreement, ask students to point to the information in the text that supports the correct answers.

Expansion/Homework
(**1**) Talk to students about what to do with unfamiliar words they encounter while reading. Encourage them to use context clues to understand what the word might mean. Have them try to identify the part of speech (noun, verb, adjective) as a way to help them understand what it might mean. Finally, encourage students to wait until they are done reading, then go back with a dictionary and look up the words. (**2**) Reading One and the exercise in Read for Main Ideas can be assigned as homework. Students can then compare their answers in class.

REACHING ALL STUDENTS: Read for Main Ideas

• **Less Proficient:** Make cloze topic sentences for students to complete.	• **More Proficient:** Have students work with a partner to develop cloze sentences for other pairs to complete.

✪✪✪ READ FOR DETAILS

If necessary, have students read the article again. Then have students complete the exercise. Go over the answers with the whole class. Ask individual students to read the details they completed. Ask them where the detail can be found in the text.

Expansion/Homework

Have students turn to the article on page 112 and cover the exercise in Read for Details. Read each statement in the exercise without giving the answer. Have students scan the text for the missing details. Explain that scanning is an important skill; it is a good way to look for specific information.

✪✪✪ MAKE INFERENCES

1. Have students complete the exercise. If the statement is false, have students write the correct statement.

2. Go over the answers as a class. If there is disagreement, have students point to the places in the article that support the correct answer.

✪✪✪ EXPRESS OPINIONS

1. Tell students that it is now their turn to express their own opinions about the topic of chain stores versus locally owned stores. Have them complete the exercise and write their opinions.

2. Divide the class into small groups and have students discuss their opinions.

CRITICAL THINKING

Give students the following questions for discussion in small groups before discussing as a whole class:

1. What is the main idea of paragraph 1?

    Answer: Large chain stores are causing small businesses to go out of business.

2. What reason was given for the small businesses to close?

    Answer: Small businesses cannot compete with large chain stores.

3. List the benefits Captain Video offers its customers. Give one example of each.

    Answer: Selection—They have more videos. Service—They give personal service. Price—They offer great discounts and longer rental times.

4. Who is the audience addressed in this newsletter?

    Answer: Customers of the video store

5. What was the purpose of the letter, to compare or to persuade? Give one example to support your answer.

    Answer: The purpose of the letter was to persuade. An example is, "Only YOU can stop the chain stores from changing Stamford."

If students are also using the companion text, you might want to have them write a short paragraph in which they agree or disagree with this statement: *Competition between businesses makes them more creative.*

✪✪✪ B READING TWO: About BLOCKBUSTER Total Access™

📁 Go to www.mynorthstarlab.com to read and listen to *About BLOCKBUSTER Total Access™*.

Suggested Time: 15 minutes

Reading Two is an excerpt from a website that describes an online service offered by Blockbuster. The reading gives students the opportunity to expand their knowledge about different types of businesses.

1. Ask students if they ever order DVDs for rental online. If so, have them describe how and why. If not, ask them if they would be interested in ordering DVDs online and why. Explain that several companies offer an online service of ordering movies. They will read about one service.

2. Have students read the text in **Exercise 1** individually. Move around the room and help with any difficult vocabulary. You can also choose to play the recording of the reading and have students listen as they read.

3. Have students complete **Exercise 2**. Go over the answers as a class.

✪✪✪ C INTEGRATE READINGS ONE AND TWO

◖ SKILLS

Organize information from the readings in a chart; synthesize information from the readings to complete a conversation.

STEP 1: Organize   Suggested Time: 15 minutes

1. Point to the chart and explain the set up with the class.

2. Divide the class into pairs and have students complete the exercise.

3. Match two pairs of students and have them compare their answers.

4. Go over the answers as a class.

STEP 2: Synthesize   Suggested Time: 20 minutes

1. Keep students together with their partners from the previous exercise.

2. Explain that they are going to have a conversation based on the information in the chart they completed in Step 1. One student will be a customer at Captain Video; the other will be the owner of Captain Video. Tell students that they should make the conversation as natural as possible.

3. Have pairs complete the conversation, then practice it for a few minutes. Move around the room and provide help where necessary.

4. Invite a few pairs to come up and act out their conversations for the class.

Expansion/Homework
Encourage students to continue the conversation beyond the lines on the page.

 Go to www.mynorthstarlab.com for *Notetaking* and *Academic Skills Practice*.

③ FOCUS ON WRITING

Ⓐ VOCABULARY

◖ SKILLS

Review vocabulary from Readings One and Two; apply vocabulary learned in the unit to a new context—a movie review; expand vocabulary by identifying word forms; use new vocabulary creatively by writing a paragraph about a business.

✪ REVIEW   Suggested Time: 15 minutes

 Go to www.mynorthstarlab.com for *Review*.

1. Ask if anyone is familiar with the movie *You've Got Mail*. If so, have that student summarize it for the class. If not, give a brief summary based on the reading on page 118.

2. Have students complete the exercise.

3. Call on students to take turns reading the completed review.

Expansion/Homework
As you review the answers, you might want to have students identify the parts of speech of the missing words.

✪✪ EXPAND   Suggested Time: 15 minutes

1. Remind students that one word can have multiple forms. Some words are spelled the same for each form; some words change the way they are spelled. Write *benefit*, *beneficial*, and *benefit* on the board. Explain that the words have the same root but different endings for a noun and adjective.

2. Have students analyze the chart. Then complete the first statement in item 1 with the class. Finally, have students complete the exercise.

3. Go over the answers with the class. Explain the answers if necessary.

VOCABULARY EXPANSION: Prefixes and Suffixes

Copy the chart below on the board. Introduce the meaning of each prefix and suffix. Ask students to submit additional words to expand the example column. As a whole group, write a paragraph using as many words with prefixes and suffixes as possible. Next, have students write their own paragraphs.

Prefix	Meaning	Example
bi– mis– re–	two wrong, bad back, again	**bi**cycle **mis**take **re**do

Suffix	Meaning	Example
–er, –or –ly –ness	person, thing in the manner of state, condition	teach**er** friend**ly** kind**ness**

✪ CREATE

Suggested Time: 20 minutes

1. Explain to students that they will write a short paragraph about a store, restaurant, or business they know.

2. Have students write their paragraphs individually and then exchange papers with a partner who will check the sentences for errors.

3. Call on individual students to read their paragraphs to the class.

Expansion/Homework
You can assign the paragraph for homework.

 Go to www.mynorthstarlab.com for additional *Vocabulary* practice.

✱✱ B GRAMMAR: *There is / There are*

Go to www.mynorthstarlab.com for *Grammar Chart* and *Exercise 2*.

☾ SKILLS

Learn *there is/there are* in sentences and *yes/no* questions.

Suggested Time: 30 minutes

1. Have students read the e-mail in **Exercise 1**. Alternatively, you can ask individual students to take turns reading the e-mail aloud. Then have students answer the questions. Go over the answers with the class.

2. Go over the chart with the class. Elicit a few example sentences.

3. Have students complete **Exercise 2**. Go over the answers with the class.

4. Have students work with a partner to complete **Exercise 3**. Students each write questions and then exchange books for students to write answers to their partner's questions.

5. Call on individual students to read their questions and answers to the class.

Expansion/Homework

For further practice, offer exercises from *Focus on Grammar 1*, 2nd Edition or Azar's *Basic English Grammar*, 3rd Edition. See the Grammar Book References on page 226 of the student book for specific units and chapters.

 Go to www.mynorthstarlab.com for additional *Grammar* practice.

C WRITING

If you wish to assign a different writing task than the one in this section, see page 129. The Alternative Writing Topics can also be assigned as additional writing topics for homework. The alternative topics relate to the theme of the unit, but they may not target the same grammar or rhetorical structures taught in the unit.

◖ SKILLS

Draw a map as a pre-writing activity; use space order; integrate the concepts, vocabulary, grammar, and rhetorical structures from the unit to write a description of a place.

✺✺✺ PREPARE TO WRITE: Drawing a Map

Suggested Time: 20 minutes

1. Explain to students that as a culminating activity, they will write a description of their favorite place. Go over the information in the task box with the class.

2. Have students think of places they like and list them in **Exercise 1**. Have students share their lists with a partner.

3. Have students look at the map in **Exercise 2** and take turns asking and answering questions about The Big Salad.

4. Review the instructions for **Exercise 3** with the class. Then have each student choose one place from his or her list to write about and draw a map.

5. For **Exercise 4**, have students work with a partner and ask questions about each other's maps. This exercise will help students clarify what they want to write about.

✪✪✪ WRITE: A Description of a Place

Suggested Time: 40 minutes

1. Read the short introduction with the class. Ask students if they have ever read a description of a place. Ask what kinds of words make the description clear. Write students' responses on the board.

2. Have students complete **Exercise 1**. Go over the answers with the class.

3. Have students reread the paragraph and complete the list in **Exercise 2**. Call on students to read their lists to the class. Encourage students to add words that are not mentioned in the paragraph but would work in the description.

4. Have students complete **Exercise 3**. Move around the room and provide assistance where necessary. Then go over the answers as a class.

5. Go over the instructions for **Exercise 4**. Have students write their first drafts. Move around the room and offer assistance if necessary. You can also assign writing the first draft for homework.

✪✪✪ REVISE: Describing a Place Using Space Order

Suggested Time: 20 minutes

1. Go over the introduction and the information in the box with the class. Explain that describing a place using space ordering makes a clear picture for the reader. Some ways to describe are up to down, left to right, around, or across.

2. Have students complete **Exercise 1** and compare their answers with a partner's.

3. Have students look back to the map on page 125 and complete the sentences in **Exercise 2**. Go over the answers with the class.

4. Go over the instructions for **Exercise 3**. Have students look at the first drafts of their paragraphs and add one to two space descriptions.

Expansion/Homework

For homework, have students write *yes/no* questions using *there is/there are* about the places on the map on page 125.

✪✪✪ EDIT: Writing the Final Draft

Suggested Time: 20 minutes

Have students write the final drafts of their paragraphs. Encourage them to use language and grammar from the unit. Make sure they go through the checklist before submitting their final drafts. Collect the paragraphs and correct them before the next class.

Link to *NorthStar: Listening and Speaking 1*

If students are also using the companion text, have them write a paragraph about each of the Google locations (New York and California).

Go to www.mynorthstarlab.com for *Writing the Final Draft.*

✪ ALTERNATIVE WRITING TOPICS

These topics give students an alternative opportunity to explore and write about issues related to the unit theme.

✪ RESEARCH TOPICS

Suggested Time: 20–30 minutes in class

1. Have students turn to page 221. Review the instructions for the activity with the class.

2. Have students complete their interviews and write a paragraph about the business they have researched.

3. In class, have students read their paragraphs to the class.

 Go to www.mynorthstarlab.com for *Student Writing Models, Integrated Task, Video Activity, Internet Activity,* and *Unit 6 Achievement Test.*

UNIT 7 Flying High and Low

OVERVIEW

Theme: Famous people

This unit focuses on the highs and lows of the career of Charles Lindbergh. Using the facts from Lindbergh's life and achievements, students explore the topic of success and failure and share their own experiences. They also write a descriptive essay about a trip.

Reading One: *Lindbergh Did It!* is a newspaper article describing Lindbergh's historic trip across the Atlantic.

Reading Two: *Timeline of Lindbergh's Life* shows the events of Lindbergh's life chronologically.

Critical Thinking

Describe an illustration
Classify information
Support answers with information
   from the text

Relate information from the unit to personal
   experiences
Support inferences
Hypothesize another's point of view

Reading

Predict content
Identify main ideas
Read for details
Make inferences

Read a timeline
Express opinions
Organize and synthesize information from the
   readings

Writing

Write sentences
Complete a diary
Make a timeline

Write an autobiography
Use time order words
Write a paragraph about a trip

Vocabulary

Define words
Use context clues to find meaning
Identify synonyms

Grammar

The simple past

📁 ***MyNorthStarLab***
Readiness Check, Background and
Vocabulary, Readings One and Two,
Notetaking and Academic Skills Practice,
Vocabulary and Grammar, Writing the
Final Draft, Achievement Test

⌾ ***Northstar: Listening and Speaking 1***
Unit 7 presents two people who work to
improve the lives of others—Wangari
Maathai and Rigoberta Menchu.

1 FOCUS ON THE TOPIC

◀ SKILLS

Describe an illustration; activate prior knowledge; share experiences; analyze new vocabulary.

✪✪✪ A PREDICT

Suggested Time: 10 minutes

1. Have students study the illustration for a minute or two. Explain any vocabulary if necessary.

2. Discuss the questions as a class. Elicit responses from students and write them on the board.

✪✪ B SHARE INFORMATION

Suggested Time: 20 minutes

1. Read the instructions for **Exercise 1** with the class. Write the phrases *high point* and *low point* on the board. Ask students to give you examples of events in one's life that could be considered high points and low points.

2. Ask students to look at the list of people in the box. If they recognize any, ask what they are famous for. As they offer ideas, ask if that was a high point or low point in their lives.

3. Have students work in pairs to complete the activity. Go over the answers as a class.

4. Have students work with a partner to complete **Exercise 2**. Then have each student report on what he or she learned about his or her partner.

Expansion/Homework
(1) As a follow-up game, you could have each student write two sentences about a celebrity describing the high points and low points of that celebrity's career. Students can read their sentences to the class without giving the identity of the celebrity. Can the class guess who the celebrity is? (2) For homework, you could have students write the information they learn in their interviews in a brief report. They can write one paragraph describing their partner's high point and one paragraph describing the low point.

Link to *NorthStar: Listening and Speaking 1*

If students are also using the companion text, you might want to have them describe the high and low points of Wangari Maathai and Rigoberta Menchu.

 C BACKGROUND AND VOCABULARY

📁 Go to www.mynorthstarlab.com for *Background and Vocabulary*.

Suggested Time: 20 minutes

1. Go over the vocabulary words as a class. Review by asking questions. For example: *Who flies an airplane? (a pilot)*

2. Have students complete the exercise. Call on students to read the completed text to the class. Correct errors if necessary.

📁 Go to www.mynorthstarlab.com for additional *Background and Vocabulary* practice.

 **FOCUS ON READING**

◖ SKILLS

Predict content; identify main ideas; read for details; make inferences; express opinions about Charles Lindbergh; read and interpret a timeline.

A READING ONE: Lindbergh Did It!

📁 Go to www.mynorthstarlab.com to read and listen to *Lindbergh Did It!*

Suggested Time: 20 minutes

Reading One is a newspaper article, in which students read about Charles Lindbergh's trans-Atlantic flight. The style is somewhat formal.

1. Ask students to look at the illustration (contest poster). Check their comprehension by asking: *How much does the winner get? Where does the pilot fly?*

2. Ask students the name of the ocean between Europe and the United States (the Atlantic ocean). Ask if any of them have flown across the ocean. If yes, how long did it take? If no, how long do they think it would take? Explain that the illustration is for a competition to fly across the Atlantic Ocean in 1927.

3. Explain that some people called Lindbergh "The Flying Fool." Explain that a fool is a person who is crazy or not intelligent. Discuss with the class why people would have said that about Charles Lindbergh.

4. Have students check the statements in **Exercise 1**. Call on students to read their answers to the class. Tell students that there are no right or wrong answers since these are only predictions.

5. Finally, have students read the article in **Exercise 2**. The reading can be assigned as homework or lab work using MyNorthStarLab. You can also choose to play the recording of the reading and have students listen as they read.

READING STRATEGY: Visualization

1. What pictures do you see in your mind as you read? Tell students how you personally reflect on reading by highlighting strong visual words, marking a detailed description, or sharing it with others. Conduct a guided visualization. Students close their eyes and create images in their mind as you create a setting, character, or an event.

   For example, you can conduct this guided visualization: *Close your eyes or put your head down. Listen to the words and try to imagine them in your mind. You are standing on a very high mountain. All you can see is white, puffy clouds and clear blue sky. You step off the cliff and instead of falling, you fly. You are weightless. Looking around you, you see birds passing you by. The wind carries you lightly as you float to the ground. You stand to walk, but your legs feel weak. Do you walk back up the mountain to try again?*

2. Discuss students' visions. Ask questions about sensory perceptions. Extend the question by inquiring if the words in the text guided that sensation. Begin reading the text to students, pausing to reflect. Perform a think-aloud as you read to verbalize thoughts, questions, and connections. Talk about what you see, hear, smell, and feel as you read. What words helped you see something more clearly?

✪✪✪ READ FOR MAIN IDEAS   Suggested Time: 10 minutes

1. Have students complete the exercise individually. Go over the answers as a class. If there is any disagreement, ask students to point to the parts in the text that support the correct answers.

2. Have students look back at their predictions on page 134. Ask them if their predictions were correct.

Expansion/Homework

Reading One and the exercise in Read for Main Ideas can be assigned as homework. Students can then compare their answers in class.

REACHING ALL STUDENTS: Read for Main Ideas

| • **Less Proficient:** Allow students to draw and label a picture to illustrate the historic trip. | • **More Proficient:** In addition to drawing an illustration, have students add statements from the text that created the image. |

✪✪✪ READ FOR DETAILS
Suggested Time: 15 minutes

1. Remind students of the difference between main ideas and details. Explain that details support the main ideas of a text. Numbers, such as person's age, are details.

2. If necessary, have students read the article again. Then do the first item as a class. Ask what the main idea is (Lindbergh's age), and ask what the detail is (his exact age, 25).

3. Have students complete the exercise. Call on individual students to read their answers to the class.

✪✪✪ MAKE INFERENCES
Suggested Time: 15 minutes

1. Explain to students that the answers to the questions are not written in the article but can be "guessed" based on what is written.

2. Divide the class into small groups. Have each student write at least two answers to the question and then share them with other group members.

3. Call on individual students to read their answers to the class.

✪✪✪ EXPRESS OPINIONS
Suggested Time: 15 minutes

1. Tell students that it is now their turn to express their own opinions about Charles Lindbergh.

2. Look at the list of words in Express Opinions. Go over the words as a class. Give an example of each word to describe a person.

3. Divide the class into pairs. Have pairs look at the list of words and discuss which word describes Charles Lindbergh.

4. Ask for volunteers to share their words and reasons with the class.

Expansion/Homework
For homework, have students write a short paragraph describing Charles Lindbergh, using the words from the list.

 ### Link to *NorthStar: Listening and Speaking 1*
If students are also using the companion text, you might want to have them repeat the exercise and choose one word that describes Wangari Maathai and Rigoberta Menchu.

CRITICAL THINKING

Give students the following questions for discussion in small groups before discussing as a whole class:

1. What record did Lindbergh set?

   Answer: He set the record for the longest non-stop flight.

2. Lindbergh's nickname before the flight was "The Flying Fool." What was his nickname after the flight?

Answer: His nickname after the flight was "Lucky Lindy."

3. What does *flew solo* mean?

Answer: It means he flew alone.

4. Why was Lindbergh flying to Paris?

Answer: He was flying to Paris because he was in a contest.

5. What questions would you ask in an interview with Charles Lindbergh?

Answers will vary, but students should be guided by the information in the text.

✪✪✪ B   READING TWO: Timeline of Lindbergh's Life

Go to www.mynorthstarlab.com to read and listen to *Timeline of Lindbergh's Life*.

Suggested Time: 20 minutes

Reading Two is a timeline that outlines events in Lindbergh's life. The reading expands students' knowledge about Charles Lindbergh. It also provides practice with reading a timeline and drawing information from a timeline.

1. Explain that a timeline is a description of events in a person's life, organized chronologically.

2. Have students read the timeline in **Exercise 1** individually. Move around the room and help with any difficult vocabulary. You can also choose to play the recording of the reading and have students listen as they read.

3. Go over any difficult vocabulary. Help students with pronunciation as needed.

4. Have students complete **Exercise 2**. Call on individual students to read their lists to the class. Write students' ideas on the board.

Expansion/Homework
For homework, have students make a timeline of their lives. In class, divide the students into small groups and have them share their timelines.

✪✪✪ C   INTEGRATE READINGS ONE AND TWO

◖ SKILLS

Organize information from the readings in a chart; synthesize information from the readings to complete a personal diary.

STEP 1: Organize
Suggested Time: 15 minutes

1. Point to the chart and explain the two columns (high and low points in Lindbergh's life). Go over the examples. Elicit one more example for each column.

2. Have students complete the exercise and share their answers with the class.

 Link to NorthStar: Listening and Speaking 1
If students are using the companion text, you might want to have them make a chart summarizing the high and low points of the lives of Wangari Maathai and Rigoberta Menchu.

STEP 2: Synthesize
Suggested Time: 15 minutes

1. Ask students what a diary is (a personal journal or record of events in one's life). Ask if any students keep or have ever kept a diary.

2. Explain that they are going to imagine they are Charles Lindbergh and are writing in his diary.

3. Look at the beginning of the diary on page 139. Read aloud while students follow along.

4. Have students complete the exercise. Remind them to use the information from the chart in Step 1. Then call on individual students to read their diaries to the class.

Expansion/Homework
You can assign Step 2 for homework. Go over the answers in class.

Go to www.mynorthstarlab.com for *Notetaking* and *Academic Skills Practice*.

③ FOCUS ON WRITING

Ⓐ VOCABULARY

◖ SKILLS

Review vocabulary from Readings One and Two; apply vocabulary learned in the unit to a new context—a biography of Amelia Earhart; expand vocabulary through the study of synonyms; use new vocabulary creatively by completing a diary entry.

✪ REVIEW

📁 Go to www.mynorthstarlab.com for *Review*.

1. Ask if students are familiar with Amelia Earhart. Explain that she was a female pilot in the early 1900s.

2. Have students complete the exercise.

3. Go over the answers with the class. Encourage students to explain what context clues helped them choose the correct answers.

✪✪ EXPAND

Suggested Time: 15 minutes

1. Go over the information about synonyms with the class. Then model the example by having students return to the reading to identify the synonyms.

2. Have students complete the exercise individually. Then go over the answers with the class.

VOCABULARY EXPANSION: Using a Thesaurus

Write the following example on the board:

Adjective	Better	Best
good	satisfactory	sufficient

For the first word, discuss the meaning and brainstorm a list of other, more interesting words that have the same meaning. When students have exhausted their ideas, demonstrate how to use a thesaurus. Then ask students to evaluate the following words for their descriptive value: *big, beautiful, cold, easy, happy, old, rich, smart, nice,* and *strong.* Point out that for the word *good, satisfactory* is a better word but *sufficient* might be the best. Students should work in small groups to repeat the procedure for the other adjectives. Return to the whole class and discuss the assigned values.

✪ CREATE

Suggested Time: 20 minutes

1. Explain to students that they will write a diary entry using a set of notes. The notes are incomplete sentences; they are ideas that students will form into sentences.

2. Go over the notes as a class and explain any difficult vocabulary.

3. Read the first note, and then write it as a complete sentence on the board. Show how the note can be made into a full sentence.

4. Have students work individually to complete the diary entry. Encourage them to use vocabulary from Review and Expand.

5. Call on individual students to read their diaries to the class.

Expansion/Homework

You might want to assign the exercise as homework, and then use class time to have students share their entries with the class.

 Go to www.mynorthstarlab.com for additional *Vocabulary* practice.

✹✹ B GRAMMAR: The Simple Past

 Go to www.mynorthstarlab.com for *Grammar Chart* and *Exercise 2.*

◀ SKILLS

To learn the simple past tense in sentences, *yes/no* questions, and *wh-* questions.

Suggested Time: 30 minutes

1. Read the paragraphs in **Exercise 1** as a class, and have students underline simple past verbs. Then have them answer the questions. Go over the answers with the class. Write the regular and irregular verbs in two columns on the board.

2. Go over the information in the chart. Elicit additional examples from students and write them on the board.

3. Have students complete **Exercise 2**. Call on students to take turns reading the completed paragraphs aloud. Correct any errors.

4. Have students complete **Exercise 3**. Call on individual students to read their questions to the class. Correct any errors.

5. If time allows, have students mingle in the room and take turns asking and answering each other's questions.

Expansion/Homework

(**1**) You can assign Exercises 2 and 3 for homework. Go over the answers in class. (**2**) For further practice, offer exercises from *Focus on Grammar 1,* 2nd Edition or Azar's *Basic English Grammar*, 3rd Edition. See the Grammar Book References on page 226 of the student book for specific units and chapters.

 Go to www.mynorthstarlab.com for additional *Grammar* practice.

C WRITING

If you wish to assign a different writing task than the one in this section, see page 150. The Alternative Writing Topics can also be assigned as additional writing topics for homework. The alternative topics relate to the theme of the unit, but they may not target the same grammar or rhetorical structures taught in the unit.

◖ SKILLS

Make a timeline; write an autobiographical story; use time order words and put events in time order; integrate the concepts, vocabulary, grammar, and rhetorical structures from the unit to write a descriptive paragraph about a trip.

✪✪✪ PREPARE TO WRITE: Making a Timeline

Suggested Time: 15 minutes

1. Explain to students that as a culminating activity, they will write a paragraph about a trip they took. Go over the information in the task box with the class.

2. Have students read the information about timelines and then complete **Exercise 1**. Have students share their lists with a partner, giving a very brief description of each entry. Encourage students to ask questions about the trips.

3. Have students read the travel diary in **Exercise 2** and think about one memorable trip they want to write about.

4. For **Exercise 3**, have students work individually to make a timeline of their memorable trip. Encourage them to include as many events as they can. Move around the room and offer assistance if necessary.

✪✪✪ WRITE: An Autobiography

Suggested Time: 40 minutes

1. Ask if anyone has read an autobiography. If so, have the student describe what it was about and how it was written. Go over the information on page 146.

2. Read the instructions for **Exercise 1** with the class. Then have students put the events in chronological order based on the information in the diary in Prepare to Write, Exercise 2. Go over the answers with the class. Finally, have them complete **Exercise 2** by writing the sentences in paragraph form.

3. Have students briefly study the travel diary in **Exercise 3** and complete the paragraph. Remind them to identify the topic sentence. Then go over the answers with the class. If there are several topic sentences offered, write them on the board and discuss which is the best and why.

4. For **Exercise 4**, have students write their first drafts. Remind them to write a topic sentence and put events in time order. They should not worry about grammar and spelling at this point. You can also assign writing the first draft for homework.

✪✪✪ REVISE: Using Time Order Words

Suggested Time: 20 minutes

1. Ask students if they know any words that show time order. If so, write them on the board. Then go over the information and the examples on page 148.

2. Have students complete **Exercise 1** and underline the time order words in the paragraph about the trip to Florida on page 147. Call on students to read their underlined words.

3. Go over the answers with the class.

4. Have students study the travel diary in **Exercise 2** briefly and then complete the paragraph. Then call on students to read their answers to the class.

5. Go over the instructions for **Exercise 3**. Have students look at the first drafts of their paragraphs and underline any time words. Tell students that they should ask themselves if the order is clear. If not, they should add or change time order words to make the order of events clear.

Expansion/Homework
As an alternative, instead of having the students evaluate their own drafts, have students exchange paragraphs and peer-correct. The other student then would determine if the order of events is clear and suggest words to add.

✪✪✪ EDIT: Writing the Final Draft

Suggested Time: 20 minutes

Have students write the final drafts of their paragraphs. Encourage them to use language and grammar from the unit. Make sure they go through the checklist before submitting their final drafts. Collect the paragraphs and correct them before the next class.

 Link to *NorthStar: Listening and Speaking 1*
If students are also using the companion text, you might want to have them write an autobiographical story about one of the women in Unit 7 of the *Listening and Speaking* strand.

Go to www.mynorthstarlab.com for *Writing the Final Draft.*

✪ ALTERNATIVE WRITING TOPICS

These topics give students an alternative opportunity to explore and write about issues related to the unit theme.

✪ RESEARCH TOPICS

Suggested Time: 20–30 minutes in class

1. Have students turn to page 221. Review the instructions for the activity with the class. Help students identify people they can write about. Write the names on the board. Have students choose one person to research.

2. Have students conduct their research on the Internet or in a library, complete a timeline, and write a paragraph about the person of their choice.

3. In class, divide the students into small groups and have them share their timelines and paragraphs with other students.

 Go to www.mynorthstarlab.com for *Student Writing Models, Integrated Task, Video Activity, Internet Activity,* and *Unit 7 Achievement Test.*

UNIT 8
Are We There Yet?

OVERVIEW

Theme: Driving problems

This unit focuses on issues related to traffic. Students explore the problem of traffic congestion, discuss options for possible solutions, and write a comparison and contrast paragraph using information from the unit.

Reading One: *Looking for Traffic Solutions* is a memo, in which a committee member of the Traffic Solutions Committee in New York outlines some attempts at reducing traffic in the United States and worldwide.

Reading Two: *New Yorkers Talk Traffic, Mayor in the Slow Lane* is a newspaper article reporting results of a survey of New Yorkers on relieving traffic congestion.

Critical Thinking

Interpret a picture
Conduct a survey
Compare traffic stories
Infer word meaning from context
Infer information not explicit in the text

Hypothesize another's point of view
Evaluate solutions to a problem
Support opinions with reasons
Identify and compare advantages and
    disadvantages

Reading

Predict content
Identify main ideas
Read for details
Make inferences

Express opinions
Organize and synthesize information from the
    readings

Writing

Complete a conversation
Write questions and answers
Make a chart
Compare and contrast

Put reasons in order
Write a comparison and contrast paragraph
    about the best way to get to school
    or work

Vocabulary	Grammar
Define words Use context clues to find meaning	Comparative adjectives

📁 ***MyNorthStarLab*** Readiness Check, Background and Vocabulary, Readings One and Two, Notetaking and Academic Skills Practice, Vocabulary and Grammar, Writing the Final Draft, Achievement Test	⚭ ***Northstar: Listening and Speaking I*** Unit 8 focuses on road rage and driving phobias.

Go to www.mynorthstarlab.com for the MyNorthStarLab *Readiness Check*.

FOCUS ON THE TOPIC

◖ SKILLS

Interpret a photograph; conduct a survey; infer the meaning of new vocabulary from context.

✪✪✪ A PREDICT

Suggested Time: 10 minutes

1. Ask students how they got to class today. Ask if there were any problems. If so, what? Was it easy, difficult? Did it take a long time? Why?

2. Discuss the questions as a class. Ask how many students have been in a similar situation and how they felt.

✪✪ B SHARE INFORMATION

Suggested Time: 25 minutes

1. First, have students work alone to complete the chart for themselves. Then have them stand up, mingle, and survey three other students.

2. Ask for a few volunteers to share their answers with the class.

Expansion/Homework
For a follow-up discussion, you can ask: *How can you avoid traffic? In what ways is traffic bad for your health?*

✪✪✪ C BACKGROUND AND VOCABULARY

Go to www.mynorthstarlab.com for *Background and Vocabulary*.

Suggested Time: 25 minutes

1. Have students read the e-mail in **Exercise 1** and then complete the questions that follow. Go over the answers as a class.

2. Next ask students if they know any interesting facts about travel and traffic. If so, ask them to share the facts with the class. Then have students read the travel facts in **Exercise 2**. When students are finished, ask them which facts were most surprising to them.

3. Have students complete **Exercise 3** and compare their answers with a partner's. Then go over the answers as a class.

 Go to www.mynorthstarlab.com for additional *Background and Vocabulary* practice.

FOCUS ON READING

◖ SKILLS

Predict content; identify main ideas; read for details; make inferences; express opinions about best solutions for traffic problems; read an article.

✪✪✪ Ⓐ READING ONE: Looking for Traffic Solutions

📂 Go to www.mynorthstarlab.com to read and listen to *Looking for Traffic Solutions*.

Suggested Time: 20 minutes

Reading One is a memo written by a member of a Traffic Solutions Committee in New York. In response to many traffic problems in New York, the committee is looking for solutions to improve the situation. The committee member describes traffic solutions in cities in the United States and around the world that could possibly work in New York.

1. Explain that students will read a memo. Explain that a memo is a type of writing used in an office, to communicate information. This memo is being sent to a committee that focuses on traffic problems in New York.

2. Have students check the words they think will appear in the memo. Call on individual students to read their answers. Then have students read the memo. The reading can be assigned as homework or lab work using MyNorthStarLab. You can also choose to play the recording of the reading and have students listen as they read.

READING STRATEGY: Annotating Text

1. Divide the reading into parts. Students in a home group are numbered 1 through 4. The students with the same number are assigned the same part of the reading and will become experts on that section.

2. Each student reads the assigned material. Students mark that text with questions about the information or vocabulary in the margin. Then students with the same part of the reading get together to form the expert groups. Each member of the group contributes ideas and opinions, and single key words or phrases. Finally, students return to their home groups to share and teach their piece of the reading.

✪✪✪ READ FOR MAIN IDEAS

Suggested Time: 10 minutes

Have students complete the activity individually. Go over the answers as a class. If there is any disagreement, ask students to point to the information in the text that supports the correct answer.

✪✪✪ READ FOR DETAILS

Suggested Time: 15 minutes

1. If necessary, have students read the memo again. Explain that they will now look for details in the memo. Remind students that details support the main ideas of a text. Here, the details are specific information about cities they read about.

2. Go over the example. Ask what the main idea is (think about the solutions in these cities). Explain that Seattle is an example of a city and bike lanes are the specific solution used in Seattle.

3. Encourage students to use scanning skills to quickly read through the text to find the answers. Explain that they will scan for the city name and then find the solution.

4. Have students complete the exercise. Go over the answers with the whole class.

Expansion/Homework

Have students summarize the information as a chart. Explain that a chart is a good way to see a lot of information in a simple form. Do an example by making a chart on the board with five rows and three columns. Title the left column *U.S. Cities*, title the middle column *Traffic Solutions*, and title the right-hand column *Results*. In the first column, write *Seattle, Washington*. In the middle, write *bike lanes*. In the cell on the right, write *people feel healthy* and *people don't worry* as two separate bullet points. Have students complete the chart. Then have students create a chart for international solutions.

REACHING ALL STUDENTS: Read for Details

• **Less Proficient:** Have students list the cities and their traffic solutions.	• **More Proficient:** Ask students to compare and contrast a U.S. city and an international city.

✪✪✪ MAKE INFERENCES

Suggested Time: 15 minutes

1. Ask students to think about Mr. Torres' memo and what ideas he had. Then ask them to think about which were his favorites. Ask for a few suggestions.

2. Have students work alone to choose the three favorite solutions and write them on the lines in **Exercise 1**. They should be ready to explain the choices.

3. Have students fill in the blanks in **Exercise 2** and then discuss their answers as a class. Encourage students to support their answers with information from the memo.

Are We There Yet? **85**

✪✪✪ EXPRESS OPINIONS   Suggested Time: 20 minutes

Tell students that it is now their turn to express their own opinions about the topic of traffic solutions for New York. First, have them rank the solutions in **Exercise 1**. Then have students discuss their choices with a partner using the arguments listed in **Exercise 2**.

 Link to *NorthStar: Listening and Speaking 1*

If students are also using the companion text, you might want to have them discuss which of the traffic solutions listed can help reduce road rage and why.

CRITICAL THINKING

Give students the following questions for discussion in small groups before discussing as a whole class:

1. What is the purpose of the memo?

   Answer: The purpose of the memo is to inform the committee about traffic solutions.

2. What city has bike lanes?

   Answer: Seattle, Washington, has bike lanes.

3. Why does traffic move faster in high-occupancy vehicle lanes?

   Answer: Traffic moves faster in HOV lanes because there are fewer cars.

4. Why are the people in Massachusetts not happy about the "Big Dig"?

   Answer: People in Massachusetts are not happy about the "Big Dig" because it cost more than planned.

5. What two international cities use above-ground transportation?

   Answer: São Paulo and Bangkok use above-ground transportation.

✪✪✪ Ⓑ READING TWO: New Yorkers Talk Traffic, Mayor in the Slow Lane

📁 Go to www.mynorthstarlab.com to read and listen to *New Yorkers Talk Traffic, Mayor in the Slow Lane*.

Suggested Time: 15 minutes

Reading Two is a newspaper article that reports on results of a survey of 800 New Yorkers about the city's traffic problems.

1. Ask students to look at the picture and discuss how the drivers feel and why. Then explain that they will read the results of a telephone survey with New Yorkers. Explain that a survey is a way to ask people what they think on a subject.

2. Ask students to guess how they think most New Yorkers feel about traffic and why.

86 UNIT 8

3. Have students read the article in **Exercise 1** individually. Move around the room and help with any difficult vocabulary. You can also choose to play the recording of the reading and have students listen as they read.

4. Have students complete **Exercise 2**. Go over the answers as a class.

5. Return to students' predictions about New Yorkers' feelings about traffic. Were they correct?

✪✪✪ C INTEGRATE READINGS ONE AND TWO

◖ SKILLS

Organize information from the readings in a chart; synthesize information from the readings to complete an interview.

STEP 1: Organize   Suggested Time: 10 minutes

1. Ask students to think about the problems in New York from Reading Two and the possible solutions in Reading One before they write their ideas in the chart.

2. Go over the answers with the entire class.

STEP 2: Synthesize   Suggested Time: 20 minutes

1. Explain that students are going to create a role play based on the information in the chart they completed in Step 1.

2. Divide the class into pairs and have students practice the interview with a partner. Tell them that they should make their interviews as natural as possible. Move around the room and provide help where necessary.

3. When all students are finished, invite a few pairs to act out their interviews.

 Go to www.mynorthstarlab.com for *Notetaking* and *Academic Skills Practice*.

 ③ FOCUS ON WRITING

A VOCABULARY

◖ SKILLS

Review vocabulary from Readings One and Two; apply vocabulary learned in the unit to a new context—a descriptive paragraph; use *take/get/go* in paragraph completion and questions and answers; use new vocabulary creatively by asking and answering questions.

✪ REVIEW

Suggested Time: 15 minutes

📁 Go to www.mynorthstarlab.com for *Review*.

1. Go over the words in the box and make sure students know the meaning of each word before they complete the exercise.

2. Have students complete the exercise individually. Go over the answers with the class.

Expansion/Homework

As an alternative, you can have students complete the exercise as a dictation. Have students cover the vocabulary words and fill in the exercise as you read the completed paragraph.

Link to *NorthStar: Listening and Speaking 1*

If students are also using the companion text, you might want to have them discuss these questions: *Is road rage a problem in Bangkok? Why or why not? What can drivers with road rage learn from drivers in Bangkok?*

✪✪ EXPAND

Suggested Time: 15 minutes

1. Write the following sample sentences on the board: *How long does it take you to get home? How do you get there? I go by car.* Ask the class to rephrase the questions if they can. For example: *How much time do you spend traveling home? How do you travel there? I travel by car.*

2. Go over the explanations and examples in the chart with the class. Offer additional explanation if necessary.

3. Have students work individually to complete the paragraph in **Exercise 1**. Go over the answers as a class.

4. Give students a few minutes to write answers to the questions in **Exercise** 2. Remind students to use the third-person *-s* in the answer with *it* as a subject. Then call on individual students to share their answers with the class. If you have a larger class, have students share their answers in small groups.

VOCABULARY EXPANSION: In the Future

Write the following sentences on the board:

CORRECT: *Michael will come to the party.*

INCORRECT: *Michael will comes to the party.*

1. Ask students to point out what makes the last sentence incorrect.

2. Explain that when using *will*, the simple form of the verb will follow.

3. Write two or three sentences on the board. Then change them using *will* to express the future time. Finally, rewrite the sentences using *will* as contracted *'ll*.

✪ CREATE   **Suggested Time: 25 minutes**

1. Explain to students that they will write questions and answers about commuting from home to school or work.

2. First, have students write their questions individually. Remind them to use the vocabulary from the unit.

3. Then divide the class into pairs and have students take turns asking and answering each other's questions.

4. Call on individual pairs to report about their partners to the class.

 Go to www.mynorthstarlab.com for additional *Vocabulary* practice.

✪✪ B GRAMMAR: Comparative Adjectives

 Go to www.mynorthstarlab.com for *Grammar Chart* and *Exercise 2*.

◖ SKILLS

Learn and use comparative adjectives in questions and statements.

Suggested Time: 30 minutes

1. Write the adjectives from **Exercise 1** on the board. Go over the number of syllables in each. Explain that syllables are like beats.

2. Draw two houses on the board, one larger than the other. Label them *A* and *B*. Ask students to compare the houses. Write on the board: *A is smaller than B. B is bigger than A.* Then draw a bicycle and a car. Write money symbols under them (one under a bicycle, four under a car). Ask which is more expensive to buy; then write a sample sentence: *A car is more expensive than a bicycle.*

3. Elicit the rule for comparative adjectives verbally (one syllable, add *-er*; two or more, use *more.* Use *than* in the sentence to compare.).

4. Go over the chart with the class. Ask individual students to read the explanations and the examples. Point out the spelling rule for adjectives that end in *y.*

5. Have students work with a partner to complete **Exercise 2**. Go over the answers as a class.

6. Have the same pairs complete **Exercise 3**. Invite individual students to read their paragraphs to the class.

Expansion/Homework
For further practice, offer exercises from *Focus on Grammar 1*, 2nd Edition or Azar's *Basic English Grammar*, 3rd Edition. See the Grammar Book References on page 226 of the student book for specific units and chapters.

 Go to www.mynorthstarlab.com for additional *Grammar* practice.

If you wish to assign a different writing task than the one in this section, see page 170. The Alternative Writing Topics can also be assigned as additional writing topics for homework. The alternative topics relate to the theme of the unit, but they may not target the same grammar or rhetorical structures taught in the unit.

◖ SKILLS

Make a chart to organize information for writing; list reasons and put them in order; integrate the concepts, vocabulary, grammar, and rhetorical structures from the unit to write a comparison and contrast paragraph.

✪✪✪ PREPARE TO WRITE: Making a Chart

Suggested Time: 20 minutes

1. Explain to students that as a culminating activity, they will write a paragraph about the best way to get to school or work. Go over the information in the task box with the class.

2. Go over the explanation about making a chart. Then ask students for other ways to compare (*cheap/expensive, big/small, hot/cold, crowded/quiet*).

3. Go over the chart in **Exercise 1** with the class. Elicit more advantages and disadvantages.

4. Have students work individually to complete **Exercise 2**. Move around the room and offer assistance if necessary. You might also ask for volunteers to share some ideas. This may help students who were not able to think of ideas.

5. Finally, have students complete **Exercise 3**.

✪✪✪ WRITE: A Comparison and Contrast Paragraph

Suggested Time: 40 minutes

1. Go over the explanation in the box. Then read the paragraph in **Exercise 1** as a class. Ask for volunteers to take turns reading sentences. When finished, ask students to identify the topic sentence and the reasons given in the paragraph.

2. Have students work with a partner to complete the outline in **Exercise 2**. Go over the outline as a class.

3. Have students work individually to write their own outlines. Remind them that the topic sentence is the answer to what the best way to get to work or school is. Also, remind them that they need to list three reasons and an explanation of each reason.

4. For **Exercise 3**, have students write the first drafts of their paragraphs. You can also assign writing the first draft for homework.

✪✪✪ REVISE: Putting Your Reasons in Order

Suggested Time: 25 minutes

1. Go over the list of transition words and phrases used to put reasons in order. Elicit additional words and phrases and write them on the board.

2. For **Exercise 1**, have students look at the paragraph in Exercise 1 on page 168. Have students underline the transition words that introduce reasons. Then call on individual students and ask them to read the sentences with transition words.

3. Have students read the list of reasons in **Exercise 2**. Then have students work with a partner and decide which are the three best reasons. Call on pairs to share their choices with the class. If time allows, have a short discussion about the reasons students checked.

4. Have students work with the same partner to complete the paragraph in **Exercise 3**. One way to do this exercise is for one student to read the sentence and for the other to write. Or both students say the sentences aloud and each writes his or her own paragraph. Ask for a few volunteers to read their paragraphs.

5. Have students complete **Exercise 4** and add transition words to their first drafts. Move around the room and make comments where appropriate. However, don't rewrite or offer specific alternatives to students.

✪✪✪ EDIT: Writing the Final Draft

Suggested Time: 20 minutes

Have students write the final drafts of their paragraphs. Encourage them to use language and grammar from the unit. Make sure they go through the checklist before submitting their final drafts. Collect the paragraphs and correct them before the next class.

 Link to *Northstar: Listening and Speaking 1*
If students are also using the companion text, you might want to have them write a comparison and contrast paragraph describing how reducing congestion could reduce road rage.

📁 Go to www.mynorthstarlab.com for *Writing the Final Draft.*

✪ ALTERNATIVE WRITING TOPICS

These topics give students an alternative opportunity to explore and write about issues related to the unit theme.

✪ RESEARCH TOPICS

Suggested Time: 20–30 minutes in class

1. Have students turn to page 222. Review the instructions for the activity with the class. As a whole class, brainstorm ideas students can research.

2. Have students conduct their research and write a comparison and contrast paragraph.

3. In class, have students share their paragraphs in small groups.

Go to www.mynorthstarlab.com for *Student Writing Models, Integrated Task, Video Activity, Internet Activity,* and *Unit 8 Achievement Test.*

Full House

OVERVIEW

Theme: Family
This unit focuses on the topic of large families, the rise of multiple births, and the impact a multiple birth has on a family and its children. Students explore the topic, discuss the question of how many children in a family is enough, and write an opinion paragraph using information from the unit.

Reading One: *Full House* is a newspaper article about the first family ever to have living septuplets.

Reading Two: *The Dionne Quintuplets* is a letter similar to one written by three of a famous set of quintuplets.

Critical Thinking

Analyze a picture
Compare families
Infer word meaning from context
Analyze a chart

Infer information not explicit in the text
Discuss the pros and cons of big families
Support opinions with reasons
Categorize information

Reading

Predict content
Read a chart
Identify main ideas
Read for details

Make inferences
Express opinions
Organize and synthesize information from the
    readings

Writing

Write answers to questions
Complete a letter
Interview classmates

Write follow-up questions
Write a concluding sentence
Write an opinion paragraph

Vocabulary	Grammar
Define words Use context clues to find meaning	*Should*

📁 ***MyNorthStarLab*** Readiness Check, Background and Vocabulary, Readings One and Two, Notetaking and Academic Skills Practice, Vocabulary and Grammar, Writing the Final Draft, Achievement Test	⚭ ***Northstar: Listening and Speaking 1*** Unit 9 deals with advantages and disadvantages of being an only child.

Go to www.mynorthstarlab.com for the MyNorthStarLab *Readiness Check*.

 FOCUS ON THE TOPIC

◖ SKILLS

Interpret a photograph; use prior knowledge; infer the meaning of new vocabulary from context.

✪✪✪ Ⓐ PREDICT

Suggested Time: 10 minutes

Focus students' attention on the photograph and then discuss the questions as a whole class. Ask students to predict what the unit will be about. Affirm each prediction as a possibility.

✪✪ Ⓑ SHARE INFORMATION

Suggested Time: 20 minutes

1. Have two students read the interview in **Exercise 1** aloud to the class. Explain the meaning of the word *twins* if students are not familiar with it.

2. Have students think of their family and complete **Exercise 2**. They might choose to write about their parents and siblings, or if they are married, their spouse and children. Then have them write sentences describing their family.

3. Next, divide the class into pairs. Have students take turns interviewing each other and writing their partner's questions in the spaces provided.

✪✪✪ Ⓒ BACKGROUND AND VOCABULARY

 Go to www.mynorthstarlab.com for *Background and Vocabulary*.

Suggested Time: 20 minutes

1. Ask students to read the interview with Ellen Sullivan. Have them pay special attention to the boldfaced words.

2. Have students complete the vocabulary exercise, then compare answers with a partner's. If students disagree, have them show where the answer is in the text. Then go over the answers as a class.

 Go to www.mynorthstarlab.com for additional *Background and Vocabulary* practice.

② FOCUS ON READING

◖ SKILLS

Interpret a chart; predict content; identify main ideas; read for details; make inferences; express opinions about families; read a letter.

✿✿✿ A READING ONE: Full House

📁 Go to www.mynorthstarlab.com to read and listen to *Full House*.

Suggested Time: 25 minutes

Reading One is a newspaper article about the McCaugheys, a family of ten. The McCaugheys are the first family ever to have living septuplets. The article describes the life and everyday challenges the family has faced.

1. Ask students to look at the chart in **Exercise 1**. Discuss the questions as a class.

2. For **Exercise 2**, have students look at the title of the article and predict what the article might be about. Affirm each prediction as a possibility.

3. Then have students read the article. The reading can be assigned as homework or lab work using MyNorthStarLab. You can also choose to play the recording of the reading and have students listen as they read.

4. For **Exercise 3**, have students look at the predictions they made in Exercise 2. Were they correct? Are students surprised by what they read? Why?

READING STRATEGY: *Wh-* Questions

To help students focus on important ideas and details, have them work with their partner to write *Who, What, When, Where,* and *Why* questions as they read. Then they should answer the questions with their books closed.

✿✿✿ READ FOR MAIN IDEAS   **Suggested Time: 10 minutes**

Have students complete the exercise individually. Go over the answers as a class. If there is any disagreement, ask students to point to the information in the text that supports the correct answer.

✿✿✿ READ FOR DETAILS   **Suggested Time: 15 minutes**

1. If necessary, have students read the article again. Then divide the class into pairs (of mixed fluency if possible) and have students complete the exercise. Students will need to scan the text quickly to find the information they need to

complete the sentences. Have students underline the details in the article as they find them.

2. Go over the answers with the whole class. Ask individual students to read the sentences they completed. Ask them where the detail can be found in the text.

REACHING ALL STUDENTS: Read for Details

• **Less Proficient:** List the names of the children. Name one characteristic for each.	• **More Proficient:** Have students consider the unique attributes of each child and predict what type of job would require such characteristics.

✪✪✪ MAKE INFERENCES   Suggested Time: 10 minutes

1. Tell students that they will need to answer the question based on what they read in the article. Remind them that the answer is not written in the text; they need to guess it based on what they read. Tell them to support their answers with information from the article.

2. Have students complete the exercise. Call on individual students to read their answers. Encourage discussion.

Link to *NorthStar: Listening and Speaking 1*
If students are using the companion text, you might want to have them compare the Golds' experience of parenting with the McCaugheys' experience. Ask: *What do the parents worry about? What are the benefits of each situation?*

✪✪✪ EXPRESS OPINIONS   Suggested Time: 15 minutes

1. Tell students that it is now their turn to express their own opinions about the McCaugheys and families in general.

2. Divide the class into pairs and have students discuss the questions.

3. Call on individual students to share their views with the class. Encourage discussion.

Expansion/Homework
Students can be asked to write a short opinion essay on one of the questions for homework.

CRITICAL THINKING

Give students the following questions for discussion in small groups before discussing as a whole class:

1. What are the risks of using medicine to help women become pregnant?

   Answer: The risks of using fertility drugs are that the baby might not be healthy or the possibility of a multiple birth.

2. How did the couple feel when they found out they were going to have seven babies?

Answer: They were surprised and nervous.

3. Give two examples of support the family received.

Answers may include any of the following: cooking, cleaning, taking care of the kids, a new van, clothing for five years, baby food, diapers, and a new house.

4. Why does Mikayla feel jealous sometimes?

Answer: Mikayla feels jealous sometimes because the septuplets receive a lot of attention.

5. What challenges might a family like the McCaugheys face?

Answers will vary, but students should support their responses with information from the text and from their own knowledge.

✪✪✪ Ⓑ READING TWO: The Dionne Quintuplets

📁 Go to www.mynorthstarlab.com to read and listen to *The Dionne Quintuplets*.

Suggested Time: 20 minutes

In Reading Two, students read a letter similar to one written by three of a famous set of quintuplets. It describes an unhappy childhood that included exploitation by curiosity seekers.

1. Have students look at the top picture. Discuss these questions: *Do the children look alike? Are they the same age? When was the picture taken? How do you think the lives of the girls in the picture were the same or different from the lives of the McCaughey children?* Then read the information about the Dionne sisters.

2. Have students read the letter in **Exercise 1** individually. Move around the room and help with any difficult vocabulary. You can also choose to play the recording of the reading and have students listen as they read.

3. Have students complete **Exercise 2**. Go over the answers with the class.

✪✪✪ Ⓒ INTEGRATE READINGS ONE AND TWO

◖ SKILLS

Organize information from the readings in a chart; synthesize information from the readings to complete a letter.

STEP 1: Organize   **Suggested Time: 15 minutes**

1. Have students review Readings One and Two. Then elicit one example for each category in the chart.

2. Have students complete the exercise and compare their answers with a partner's. Then call on individual students to share their answers with the class.

STEP 2: Synthesize   **Suggested Time: 20 minutes**

1. Explain that students are going to write a letter based on the information in the chart they completed in Step 1. They will write from the point of view of the McCaugheys to the Dionnes. The letter should describe the McCaugheys' life and respond to points raised in the letter from the Dionnes.

2. Start by asking pairs of students to consider what they will report on about the McCaughey family. Make a list. Then ask students to consider what they want to comment on about the Dionnes. Make a list.

3. Have students write their letters. Move around the room and provide assistance where necessary.

4. When all students are finished, invite a few volunteers to read their letters to the class.

Extension/Homework
Students can write their letters for homework. During the next class, have them share their letters in small groups.

 Link to *Northstar: Listening and Speaking 1*
If students are also using the companion text, you might want to have them write a letter as a child from a large family to an only child. Tell the only child about your life in a big family and ask about his or hers.

Go to www.mynorthstarlab.com for *Notetaking* and *Academic Skills Practice*.

3 FOCUS ON WRITING

A VOCABULARY

SKILLS

Review vocabulary from Readings One and Two; expand vocabulary by learning idioms and expressions about families; use new vocabulary creatively by writing sentences and a paragraph.

✪ REVIEW   **Suggested Time: 10 minutes**

Go to www.mynorthstarlab.com for *Review*.

Have students complete the exercise. Then ask for volunteers to write the sentences on the board. If time is limited, ask students to provide only the correct word.

1. Review what an idiom is—a group of words whose meaning cannot be determined from the individual meaning of the words. Explain that the idioms they will learn are all in reference to families.

2. Go over the idioms. Get sample sentences from students if possible. Ask if the idiom is something that applies to the student (for example: *Are you an only child? Was there sibling rivalry in your family? If so, what was it about?*).

3. Have students complete the exercise. Then ask individual students to share their answers with the class.

VOCABULARY EXPANSION: Retell the Text

Students will work in pairs to retell the story in Readings One or Two, using the target vocabulary. As Student A retells the text, Student B listens for the key words. Students reverse roles and repeat. This is a good strategy to review and retain new vocabulary.

✪ CREATE   **Suggested Time:** 20 minutes

1. Explain to students that they will write sentences about the McCaughey family and then put them in time order in a paragraph.

2. Have students work with a partner and write their sentences on a separate sheet of paper first. This will help them focus on ideas first.

3. After students have written their sentences, have them each write a paragraph. Call on individual students to read their paragraphs to the class.

Expansion/Homework
You can assign the paragraph writing as homework. Then students can share their paragraphs in small groups.

📁 Go to www.mynorthstarlab.com for additional *Vocabulary* practice.

☯☯ Ⓑ GRAMMAR: *Should*

📁 Go to www.mynorthstarlab.com for *Grammar Chart* and *Exercise 2*.

◖ SKILLS

Learn and use *should* to express opinions.

Suggested Time: 30 minutes

1. Go over the instructions for **Exercise 1** with the class. Then have two students read the conversation aloud. Finally, have students answer the questions. Go over the answers as a class.

2. Go over the chart with the class. Ask individual students to read the explanations and the examples. Point out that *should* is a helping verb; there is always a main verb in the sentence. Identify the main verb in each sentence. Point out that *shouldn't* is used in negative sentences.

3. Have students complete **Exercise 2** individually and then compare answers with a partner's. Go over the answers as a class. Then have students discuss if they agree or disagree with the expert's advice and why.

4. Go over the instructions for **Exercise 3**. Stress to students that they are going to give their own advice, so there are no right or wrong answers. Have students complete the exercise and then share their opinions as a class or in small groups.

Expansion/Homework

For further practice, offer exercises from *Focus on Grammar 1*, 2nd Edition or Azar's *Basic English Grammar*, 3rd Edition. See the Grammar Book References on page 226 of the student book for specific units and chapters.

Go to www.mynorthstarlab.com for additional *Grammar* practice.

C WRITING

If you wish to assign a different writing task than the one in this section, see page 192. The Alternative Writing Topics can also be assigned as additional writing topics for homework. The alternative topics relate to the theme of the unit, but they may not target the same grammar or rhetorical structures taught in the unit.

SKILLS

Ask follow-up questions to gather information; support opinions with reasons; write a concluding sentence; integrate the concepts, vocabulary, grammar, and rhetorical structures from the unit to write an opinion paragraph.

✪✪✪ PREPARE TO WRITE: Using Follow-Up Questions

Suggested Time: 20 minutes

1. Explain to students that as a culminating activity, they will write an opinion paragraph about multiple-birth families. Go over the information in the task box with the class.

2. Explain to students that to help them form their opinion, they will interview a classmate. Explain that while interviewing, a good way to get more information is to ask follow-up questions. Then go over the explanations and examples with the class.

3. Have students complete **Exercise 1** and compare their follow-up questions with a partner's. Encourage students to come up with several follow-up questions.

4. Divide the class into pairs and have students complete **Exercise 2**. Tell students they may ask more questions if they choose. Move around the room and offer assistance or feedback if necessary.

✪✪✪ WRITE: An Opinion

Suggested Time: 30 minutes

1. Ask if students are familiar with any phrases or words that show an opinion. Elicit some examples and write them on the board. Then go over the explanation and examples with the class.

2. Go over the paragraph in **Exercise 1** with the class. Ask for volunteers to read aloud while students follow along. Then complete the questions as a class. Emphasize the importance of giving support to make the arguments stronger.

3. Go over the instructions for **Exercise 2** and have students write their first drafts. You can also assign writing the first draft for homework.

✪✪✪ REVISE: Writing a Concluding Sentence

Suggested Time: 20 minutes

1. Go back to the concluding sentence in the paragraph on page 190. Have students identify the topic sentence as well. Have students compare the topic sentence and the concluding sentence. Then go over the explanation with the class.

2. Have students read the paragraph in **Exercise 1** individually and choose the best concluding sentence. Then have them compare their choice with a partner's and explain why. Go over the answer with the class. Point out how the concluding sentence mirrors the topic sentence. The other two options are separate ideas.

3. Explain that concluding sentences can be of a few types—repetition, opinion, or reference to the future. Then have students complete **Exercise 2** individually. Go over the answers with the class.

4. Then have students complete **Exercise 3** and write a concluding sentence for their paragraphs.

Expansion/Homework
Have students exchange drafts and look for a good concluding sentence and at least one reason for each opinion. Have students give each other verbal feedback on these points.

✪✪✪ EDIT: Writing the Final Draft

Suggested Time: 20 minutes

Have students write the final drafts of their paragraphs. Encourage them to use language and grammar from the unit. Make sure they go through the checklist before submitting their final drafts. Collect the paragraphs and correct them before the next class.

 Link to *NorthStar: Listening and Speaking 1*
If students are also using the companion text, you might want to have them write an opinion paragraph on being an only child.

📁 Go to www.mynorthstarlab.com for *Writing the Final Draft.*

✪ ALTERNATIVE WRITING TOPICS

These topics give students an alternative opportunity to explore and write about issues related to the unit theme.

✪ RESEARCH TOPICS

Suggested Time: 20–30 minutes in class

1. Have students turn to pages 222–223. Review the instructions for the activity with the class. Help students identify websites and stores they can visit to gather information.

2. Have students complete the research and write a paragraph summarizing their findings.

3. In class, have students share their paragraphs in small groups.

📁 Go to www.mynorthstarlab.com for *Student Writing Models, Integrated Task, Video Activity, Internet Activity,* and *Unit 9 Achievement Test.*

How Young Is Too Young?

OVERVIEW

Theme: Sports

This unit focuses on the topic of sports and young people becoming professional athletes. Students explore the topic, discuss the question of how young is too young to join the world of professional sports, and write an advice letter using the information from the unit.

Reading One: *Ready Freddy?* is a newspaper article about a young athlete as he prepares to embark on the world of professional sports.

Reading Two: *Bram Tarek* is an imaginary interview with a young athlete who postpones entry into professional sports.

Critical Thinking

Interpret a picture
Compare sports preferences
Discuss the benefits and drawbacks of
        being a professional athlete
Infer word meaning from context

Infer information not explicit in the text
Support opinions with reasons
Categorize information
Hypothesize another's point of view
Express agreement and disagreement

Reading

Predict content
Identify main ideas
Read for details
Make inferences

Express opinions
Organize and synthesize information from the
        readings

Writing

Complete an interview
Complete sentences
Write a dialogue based on pictures

Brainstorm
Give strong advice
Write a response giving advice

Vocabulary	Grammar
Define words	*Very, too,* and *enough*
Use context clues to find meaning	
Use idiomatic expressions	

📁 *MyNorthStarLab*
Readiness Check, Background and Vocabulary, Readings One and Two, Notetaking and Academic Skills Practice, Vocabulary and Grammar, Writing the Final Draft, Achievement Test

⬭ *Northstar: Listening and Speaking 1*
Unit 10 focuses on the world's most popular sport, soccer.

Go to www.mynorthstarlab.com for the MyNorthStarLab *Readiness Check.*

FOCUS ON THE TOPIC

◀ SKILLS

Interpret a picture; compare sports preferences; use prior knowledge; infer the meaning of new vocabulary from context.

✸✸✸ A PREDICT

Suggested Time: 10 minutes

1. Focus students' attention on the picture. Call on individual students to describe what they see and predict what the unit will be about. Affirm each prediction as a possibility.

2. Ask if any students have had similar dreams.

✸✸ B SHARE INFORMATION

Suggested Time: 15 minutes

1. Ask students why they think sports are popular (for example, national unity, tradition, exercise, etc.). Then ask them what sports are popular in their country, city, school, or family.

2. Go over the questions with the class. Be sure to define the term *professional athlete.*

3. Divide the class into pairs and have them have discuss the questions. Move around the room and ask additional questions. Provide help with vocabulary where necessary. Then ask for volunteers to share their answers.

✸✸✸ C BACKGROUND AND VOCABULARY

Go to www.mynorthstarlab.com for *Background and Vocabulary.*

Suggested Time: 20 minutes

1. Ask students to read the text in **Exercise 1**. Discuss with students if they are familiar with any of the athletes. Add any information they know.

2. Have students complete **Exercise 2** individually. Go over the answers with the class.

Have students bring in pictures of their favorite athletes and tell the class what they know of their background.

📁 Go to www.mynorthstarlab.com for additional *Background and Vocabulary* practice.

② FOCUS ON READING

◖ SKILLS

Make predictions; identify main ideas; read for details; make inferences; express opinions about becoming a professional athlete at a young age; read an interview.

✹✹✹Ⓐ READING ONE: Ready Freddy?

📁 Go to www.mynorthstarlab.com to read and listen to *Ready Freddy?*

Suggested Time: 20 minutes

Reading One is a newspaper article about Freddy Adu, a high school student who is going to become a professional soccer player. Students read about how Adu is preparing to enter the world of professional sports.

1. Have students read the title of the article and the caption and check the statement in **Exercise 1** that best describes what the article will be about. Call on students to share their answers with the class.

2. Have students read the article in **Exercise 2**. The reading can be assigned as homework or lab work using MyNorthStarLab. You can also choose to play the recording of the reading and have students listen as they read.

3. For **Exercise 3**, ask students if their predictions were confirmed by reading the text. If not, ask students to share what they had assumed.

READING STRATEGY: Summarization

Explain to students that a summary briefly restates the main points of a text. Give students ample opportunity to discuss and write about the information presented in order to process it. Ask students to work in pairs to read and write. Student A reads a paragraph to Student B. Student B will state the subject of the text and tell what is happening (Who is this mainly about and what action is it mainly about?). Each person will then use this subject and predicate to write his or her own summary sentence. Students reverse roles and continue reading.

Have students complete the exercise individually. Go over the answers as a class. If there is any disagreement, ask students to point to the information in the text that supports the correct answers.

REACHING ALL STUDENTS: Read for Main Ideas	
• **Less Proficient:** Have students summarize small chunks of the text.	• **More Proficient:** Have students seek additional information on the subject to extend their knowledge. Tell them to use main ideas to create a summary of the new information.

✿✿✿ **READ FOR DETAILS**   **Suggested Time: 15 minutes**

1. If necessary, have students read the article again. Then have them complete the exercise. Encourage them to underline the information in the text that supports the answers.

2. Go over the answers with the whole class. Ask individual students to read the details they completed. Ask students where the detail can be found in the text.

Expansion/Homework
Ask students to take notes while reading, and then ask them to try and complete both exercises using their notes alone. Then allow students to return to the text to check their answers and/or fill in any gaps in the exercises.

✿✿✿ **MAKE INFERENCES**   **Suggested Time: 10 minutes**

1. Explain that students just read about various approaches to professional sports—the coaches, the players, the media, the school, and the sponsors all have different goals. Students will need to decide what these goals are, based on what they read in the article.

2. Have students complete the exercise. Encourage them to use the text to support their ideas. Then go over the answers as a class.

✿✿✿ **EXPRESS OPINIONS**   **Suggested Time: 15 minutes**

1. Tell students that it is now their turn to express their own opinions about the topic of young people becoming professional athletes.

2. Focus students' attention on the chart. Explain that *it depends* means that your answer could be *agree* or *disagree* depending on a situation. It is less strong than *agree* or *disagree*, and it is not definite.

3. Have students complete the chart and share their opinions with a partner. Students must support their opinions with reasons. Their partner must ask at least one follow-up question.

Give students the following questions for discussion in small groups before discussing as a whole class:

1. Why does Freddy Adu attend Edison Academic Center?

   Answer: Edison is a school for students with special talents in sports or art.

2. What sport does Roy Williams play?

   Answer: He plays professional football in the United States for the Dallas Cowboys.

3. Why is Adu working in a preschool?

   Answer: He is working in a preschool to learn responsibility.

4. What do the coaches advise Adu to do about untrue and unkind comments?

   Answer: They advise him not to get angry.

5. What advice would you give to 14-year-old Adu when he graduates?

   Answers will vary.

✪✪✪ B READING TWO: Bram Tarek

Go to www.mynorthstarlab.com to read and listen to *Bram Tarek*.

Suggested Time: 15 minutes

Reading Two is an imaginary interview with a college student who decided to wait before becoming a professional basketball player in order to finish college.

1. Have students read the title. Explain that *pros* means professional sports. Before they read, ask students to predict why Bram Tarek might be saying no to the pros.

2. Have students read the interview in **Exercise 1**. Move around the room and help with any difficult vocabulary. You can also choose to play the recording of the reading and have students listen as they read. Then go over students' predictions. Were they correct?

3. Have students work individually to complete **Exercise 2** and then compare their answers with a partner's. Finally, go over the answers with the class.

4. If time allows, discuss with students if they think Bram Tarek made the right decision.

◖ SKILLS

Organize information from the readings in a chart; synthesize information from the readings to write an interview.

STEP 1: Organize   **Suggested Time: 15 minutes**

1. Tell students that they will need to use the information from Readings One and Two to complete the chart. Then divide the class into pairs and have them complete the exercise.

2. Call on pairs to share their answers with the class.

STEP 2: Synthesize   **Suggested Time: 20 minutes**

1. Have students work with the same partner. Explain that they are going to conduct an interview based on the information in the chart they completed in Step 1.

2. Have students write their interviews and then practice them for a few minutes.

3. Call on pairs to role-play their interviews for the class. Encourage students to be as natural as possible.

 Go to www.mynorthstarlab.com for *Notetaking* and *Academic Skills Practice*.

⌾③ FOCUS ON WRITING

A VOCABULARY

◖ SKILLS

Review vocabulary from Readings One and Two; expand vocabulary by learning idioms and expressions about sports; use new vocabulary creatively by completing an interview.

✺ REVIEW   **Suggested Time: 10 minutes**

Go to www.mynorthstarlab.com for *Review*.

1. Go over the example with the class. Explain that one word in each item does not make sense.

2. Have students complete the exercise. Then go over the answers with the class.

✪✪ EXPAND

Suggested Time: 15 minutes

1. Review the meaning of idioms if necessary. Explain that these are sports related, but people use them in everyday life as well.

2. Have individual students read the idioms and examples in **Exercise 1** aloud. Encourage students to offer other example sentences. Ask students if they know any other idioms that are related to sports but can be used in everyday life as well.

3. Have students work individually to complete **Exercise 2**. Then go over the answers with the class.

Expansion/Homework
For homework, have students write additional sentences with the idioms.

Link to *NorthStar: Listening and Speaking 1*
If students are also using the companion text, you might want to have them write additional sentences with the idioms from the *Listening and Speaking* strand.

VOCABULARY EXPANSION: The Way of Words

1. Write the following quote by H.G. Wells on the board and ask students to consider the meaning: "A new word is like a wild animal. You must learn its ways before you can use it."

2. Lead a discussion about the ways you can learn a word. Guide students to realize that not until they have manipulated the word and used it in their own speech and writing do they possess that word. Students' ideas may include: display words with definitions and illustrations, look up a word in the dictionary and record a definition, use context clues in the sentence, analyze features of the word, categorize the word, repeat exposure to the word.

3. Present a list of 5–10 new words from the text. Then ask students to use the ideas suggested to *know* a word well enough to write a sentence of their own to help the reader understand its meaning.

✪ CREATE

Suggested Time: 25 minutes

1. Go over the instructions for **Exercise 1**. Point out that it is not polite to ask people questions about how much money they make.

2. First, have students write five questions to ask in the interview. Tell them to use vocabulary from the unit. Then have students conduct the interview and write the person's answers in the space provided. Finally, have students write a paragraph summarizing what they found out about the person they interviewed. Have students share their paragraphs in small groups. You can also assign writing the paragraph for homework.

3. Have students look at the pictures in **Exercise 2** and discuss what they see. Then have them fill in the speech bubbles. Have students compare answers with a partner's. Then call on individual students to read their sentences to the class.

Go to www.mynorthstarlab.com for additional *Vocabulary* practice.

 B GRAMMAR: *Very, Too, and Enough*

Go to www.mynorthstarlab.com for *Grammar Chart* and *Exercise 2*.

◖ SKILLS

Learn proper use of *very, too,* and *enough.*

Suggested Time: 30 minutes

1. Have students complete **Exercise 1** individually. Then call on students to read the sentences that represent the meaning of each statement.

2. Look at the picture as a class. Discuss the cars. Are they expensive? The same price? Is one cheap? Do students want to buy one? Can they afford it? Then go over the information and examples in the chart. Offer additional explanation and examples if necessary.

3. Have students complete **Exercise 2**. Ask for volunteers to write sentences on the board. Correct as necessary.

4. Have students complete **Exercise 3**. Then call on individual students to read their answers with the class. If there is disagreement, have students turn to the picture and explain their answers.

5. Have students complete **Exercise 4** and share their answers in small groups.

Expansion/Homework
(1) Students can complete Exercises 2–4 at home. In class, students can share their answers in small groups. (2) For further practice, offer exercises from *Focus on Grammar 1*, 2nd Edition or Azar's *Basic English Grammar*, 3rd Edition. See the Grammar Book References on page 226 of the student book for specific units and chapters.

Go to www.mynorthstarlab.com for additional *Grammar* practice.

If you wish to assign a different writing task than the one in this section, see page 217. The Alternative Writing Topics can also be assigned as additional writing topics for homework. The alternative topics relate to the theme of the unit, but they may not target the same grammar or rhetorical structures taught in the unit.

◖ SKILLS

Brainstorm ideas for writing; give strong advice; understand the steps in giving advice; understand degrees of advice; integrate the concepts, vocabulary, grammar, and rhetorical structures from the unit to write a letter of advice.

✪✪✪ PREPARE TO WRITE: Brainstorming

Suggested Time: 15 minutes

1. Explain to students that as a culminating activity, they will write a letter of advice. Go over the information in the task box with the class.

2. Then have students read the letter from a parent to the online advice group. Explain that they will write a letter of advice in response.

3. Remind students that in brainstorming, they are supposed to generate as many ideas as possible and that all ideas are welcome. (See Unit 2 to review brainstorming.)

4. Have students work with a partner to brainstorm the pros and cons of becoming a professional athlete. After a few minutes, combine pairs into groups of four. Compare lists and have students add more items if necessary.

5. Have students individually decide what their personal opinion is. Have them think about what they will tell Diana.

✪✪✪ WRITE: A Letter of Advice

Suggested Time: 40 minutes

1. Ask students if they have ever written or received a letter of advice. Ask whom it was to or from and what happened. As a class, discuss what would be in a letter of advice (advice, reasons, etc.). Ask what they think the reader wants to see in a letter. Explain the reader is called "the audience." Then go over the steps in giving advice.

2. Have students read the letter in **Exercise 1**. Review what the problem is.

3. Have students put the sentences in **Exercise 2** in order. Explain there is no one correct order. Then have students compare answers with a partner's.

4. Have students work individually to complete **Exercise 3** and write the letter. When done, have students compare their letters with a partner's. Ask for one or two volunteers to read their letters to the class.

5. For **Exercise 4**, have students write their first drafts. Have them focus on their ideas. Be sure they support their opinions with reasons. Encourage students to use vocabulary from the unit. You can also assign writing the first draft for homework.

✪✪✪ REVISE: Giving Strong Advice

Suggested Time: 20 minutes

1. Explain that when giving advice, you can give advice of different strengths. You might or might not want to give strong advice depending on the situation and the person. There are different words to use depending on the strength of the advice.

2. Go over the different levels of advice in the graph and the chart. Have individual students volunteer to read the example sentences. Offer additional explanation and examples if necessary.

3. Have students complete **Exercise 1**. Encourage them to use all forms of advice. Then ask for volunteers to read their answers. Elicit more than one answer for some of the sentences and point out the different levels of advice.

4. Go over the instructions for **Exercise 2**. Have students look at their drafts and underline the advice they gave Diana. If they did not give advice, have them add some now. If they did, have students determine if it is strong enough, or too strong, and make changes accordingly.

✪✪✪ EDIT: Writing the Final Draft

Suggested Time: 20 minutes

Have students write the final drafts of their letters. Encourage them to use language and grammar from the unit. Make sure they go through the checklist before submitting their final drafts. Collect the letters and correct them before the next class.

Link to NorthStar: Listening and Speaking 1
If students are also using the companion text, you might want to have them write an advice column on appreciating soccer.

Go to www.mynorthstarlab.com for *Writing the Final Draft.*

✪ ALTERNATIVE WRITING TOPICS

These topics give students an alternative opportunity to explore and write about issues related to the unit theme.

✪ RESEARCH TOPICS

Suggested Time: 20–30 minutes in class

1. Have students turn to pages 223–224. Review the instructions for the activity with the class.

2. Have students conduct their research and create a timeline. Encourage students to bring in photographs of the athletes they've researched.

3. Have students display their timelines in class and share the information they've gathered.

 Go to www.mynorthstarlab.com for *Student Writing Models, Integrated Task, Video Activity, Internet Activity,* and *Unit 10 Achievement Test.*

Student Book Answer Key

UNIT 1

1A PREDICT, page 1

Suggested answers:

1. They are at their computers. One woman is in Canada. The other is in New Zealand.
2. They are e-mailing.
   They are chatting online.
3. It is a website for / about friendship.
   It is a website to make friends.
   It is a place where friends meet.

1B SHARE INFORMATION, pages 2–3

2, page 3

1. Send or read e-mail and use a search engine, like Google®
2. Buy something
3. Get news

1C BACKGROUND AND VOCABULARY, pages 3–4

1. a   6. a
2. b   7. b
3. b   8. a
4. a   9. b
5. b   10. a

READ FOR MAIN IDEAS, page 7

1. a, c   2. a, b

READ FOR DETAILS, page 7

1. 1996   5. 190
2. 20   6. 8 to 88
3. 13,000   7. 55, 45
4. 4.7 million

MAKE INFERENCES, page 7

1. Probably false. People said she was too young to help.
2. Probably true. The volunteers are probably her friends. She uses The Friendship Page herself. She seems to be very friendly.
3. Probably true. Many people use The Friendship Page.
4. Probably true. The reading explains how it is safe. It also compares it to other websites that are not as safe.

2B READING TWO, page 9

1. F   4. T
2. T   5. F
3. T

STEP 1: Organize, page 10

	The Friendship Page	MySpace®
Easy to use	Yes	Yes
Personal webpages	No	Yes
Fun	Yes	Yes
Friendly	Yes	Yes
Males and females	Yes	Yes
Users of different ages	Yes	Yes
OK to use for business	No	Yes
Safe for young users	Yes	No
Interesting pages or groups	Yes	Yes
Free for users	Yes	Yes
Problems	No¹	Yes

¹ Students may have ideas about problems not mentioned in the readings.

STEP 2: Synthesize, page 11

Answers will vary. Possible responses:

1. Do you like The Friendship Page?
   Of course I do!
   The Friendship Page is <u>fun / easy to use / friendly / etc.</u>
   It has <u>quotes / poetry / etc.</u>
   Users can <u>meet (make) new friends / get advice / etc.</u>.
2. Do you like MySpace?
   Yes, I do!
   MySpace is <u>free / exciting / popular, etc.</u>
   It has <u>many users / many groups / etc.</u>
   Users can <u>make a personal webpage / meet many people / etc.</u>
3. Is there a problem with The Friendship Page?
   Well, maybe a small one.
   The Friendship Page needs <u>money and volunteers.</u>
   We need help!
4. Is there a problem with MySpace?
   MySpace is not always <u>safe.</u>
   People need to be careful with their personal information.

REVIEW, page 12

2. community	8. quotes
3. laughed	9. Volunteers
4. peace	10. safe
5. meet	11. Users
6. chat	12. personal
7. advice	

EXPAND, pages 13–14

Answers will vary. Suggested answers:

1. You: <u>Nice to meet you</u>. My name is <u>John</u>.
   Jeff: <u>Nice to meet you</u>, too.
2. You: Oh, that's right. <u>Nice to meet / see you again</u>, Janet.
3. You: OK. <u>Nice meeting you. / Nice chatting with you. / Nice talking to you (face to face)</u>.
   Jack: You, too. Thanks. <u>Nice meeting / chatting with / talking to you</u>, too.
4. You: OK. <u>Nice talking to you / Nice chatting with you</u>. Thanks for calling.

3B GRAMMAR

2, page 16

1. Q: <u>Is</u> <u>The Friendship Page</u> a website?
   A: Yes, <u>it</u> <u>is</u>. <u>It</u> <u>is</u> a website about friendship.
2. Q: Who <u>is</u> <u>Bronwyn Polson</u>?
   A: <u>She</u> <u>is</u> a young woman from Australia.
3. Q: <u>Am</u> <u>I</u> too young to help?
   A: No, <u>you</u> <u>aren't</u>.
4. Q: <u>Does</u> <u>Bronwyn</u> <u>have</u> a lot of friends?
   A: Yes, <u>she</u> <u>does</u>. <u>She</u> <u>has</u> a lot of friends on The Friendship Page.
5. Q: <u>Do</u> <u>users</u> <u>have</u> trouble using The Friendship Page?
   A: No, <u>they</u> <u>don't</u>. <u>They</u> <u>don't have</u> trouble using it.

3, pages 17–18

1. Is The Friendship Page a website?
2. Do Friendship Page users have personal webpages?
3. Does The Friendship Page have a chat room?
4. Does Bronwyn Polson have a goal?
5. What is Bronwyn's goal?
6. How old is The Friendship Page?
7. Who is Bronwyn Polson?
8. Is Bronwyn from England?
9. Where is Bronwyn from?
10. Does Bronwyn Polson have people to help her?
11. How old are you?
12. Where are you from?
13. Do you have one best friend?
14. Who is your best friend? / Who are your best friends?
15. Do you have a personal webpage on MySpace?

Your partner's answers, page 18

Answers may vary. Suggested answers:

1. Yes, it is.
2. No, they don't.
3. Yes, it does.
4. Yes, she does.
5. Her goal is to make "peace through friendship."
6. The Friendship Page is ___ years old. (The current year minus 1996.)
7. Bronwyn Polson is a young woman from Australia. She started The Friendship Page.
8. No, she isn't.
9. She's from Australia.
10. Yes, she does. She has 20 volunteers to help her.
11. I'm ___ years old. / I'd rather not say.
12. I'm from ___.
13. Yes, I do. / No, I don't. I have more than one best friend.
14. His / Her name is ___. / Their names are _____.
15. Yes, I do. / No, I don't.

PREPARE TO WRITE, page 19

1. What is your name?
2. Where are you from?
3. When is your birthday?
4. Do you have a job? What is your job? Are you a student?
5. Do you have hobbies or interests? What are they?
6. Who is your best friend?
7. Where is he (or she) from?
8. How old is he (or she)?
9. Does your friend have a job? What is his (or her) job? Is he (or she) a student?
10. What are his (or her) hobbies or interests?

WRITE

1, page 20

What Is Facebook?

<u>Facebook</u> <u>is</u> another popular website. <u>Facebook</u> <u>started</u> in 2004. <u>It</u> <u>is</u> really great! <u>Users</u> <u>have</u> personal webpages. <u>They</u> <u>chat</u> with old friends and <u>meet</u> new ones. <u>Are</u> <u>you</u> interested? <u>Visit</u> Facebook online for more information.

2, page 21

	sentence	not a sentence
1. My friend's name is Jane[.]	___	✓
2. Urville and Vera are from Chicago.	✓	___
3. Tony [is] 23 years old.	___	✓
4. [Pam is] a good student.	___	✓
5. My sister likes playing basketball.	✓	___
6. I play basketball[.]	___	✓
7. She has a lot of friends.	✓	___

8. My brother [is] my best friend. ___ ✓

9. [We] have fun on The Friendship Page. ___ ✓

10. We like reading the jokes and the quotes. ✓ ___

3, page 21

[My] classmate's name is Bernard. He is 24 years old. He is from Senegal[.] [He likes] playing soccer and going dancing. Bernard's best friend [is] Alexandre. [He] is from France. He is intelligent and shy. He likes going to the beach and reading. Do you have any questions to ask him[?]

REVISE, page 22

4, 6

3, page 23

Description One

My classmate's name is Fernando. He is from Spain. He is 21 years old. He is a student in Chicago. Fernando is friendly. He likes going to parties. Fernando's best friend is Ricardo. (He is from Spain. He is 20 years old. He is a student in Madrid. Ricardo is friendly and athletic. He likes going to parties and playing sports.)

Description Two

My classmate's name is Fernando. His best friend is Ricardo. Fernando is from Spain. He is 21 years old. (Ricardo is also from Spain. He is 20 years old.) Fernando is a student in Chicago. (Ricardo is a student in Madrid.) Fernando and Ricardo are both friendly. They like going to parties. (Ricardo also like playing sports.)

UNIT 2

1A PREDICT, page 25

1. *Students will point to picture A.*
2. 1. school sweater, 2. skirt, 3. dress shirt, 4. blazer (also called a jacket), 5. dress pants, 6. T-shirt, 7. jacket, 8. polo shirt, 9. sweater, 10. jeans
3. *Answers will vary.*

1C BACKGROUND AND VOCABULARY, page 27

1, page 27

Most people think it's a bad idea.

2, page 28

a. comfortable   e. increase
b. fashion   f. designer
c. teams   g. expensive
d. spirit   h. neat

3, page 28

Answers may vary.

For: 3, 6, 7, 8
Against: 1, 2, 4, 5, 9
Not sure: 2, 6

2A READING ONE, page 29

Mr. Collins is telling students and parents about a uniform.

READ FOR MAIN IDEAS, page 30

c

READ FOR DETAILS, page 30

1. white, blue, gray
2. fashion
3. expensive
4. neat, comfortable
5. spirit

MAKE INFERENCES, page 30

1. F   4. F
2. T   5. F
3. T

2B READING TWO

2, page 32

1. She disagrees with him.
2. She says, "This is a bad idea." She wants people to call the principal to give their opinion.

STEP 1: Organize, page 32

For Uniforms	*Against* Uniforms
• Uniforms help students study hard. • Students will think about school, not fashion. • Uniforms are neat and clean. • Uniforms are more comfortable. • Uniforms increase school spirit. • Uniforms are less expensive.	• Some uniforms are more expensive than other clothes. • Uniforms decrease school spirits. • Uniforms decrease individuality. • Sometimes it's OK to look messy.

REVIEW, page 33

1. comfortable   6. clothes
2. fashion   7. team
3. designer   8. spirit
4. increases, decreases   9. individuality
5. neat, messy   10. expensive

EXPAND, page 34

Answers will vary. Suggested answers:

1. Every morning before breakfast, I get dressed.
2. When I feel cold in class, I put on a sweater.
3. When you play on the baseball team, you need to wear a uniform.

3B GRAMMAR

1, page 36

3 / In his letter, Mr. Collins says that students will wear a uniform starting next year.

There will be no individuality—student in uniforms all look the same and feel the same.

Next year students at Lincoln High will all look and feel the same: bad.

WRITE

3, page 39

Answers will vary. Suggested answers:

1. Free books for students is a good idea because books are expensive.
2. Fifty-minute classes are a bad idea because fifty minutes is too short.
3. Buying designer clothes is a good idea because you will feel more fashionable.
4. Wearing jeans at school is a good idea because you will feel more relaxed.
5. A police officer in a uniform is a good idea because people can find them easily.
6. A waitress in a uniform is a good idea because their regular clothes won't get dirty.

UNIT 3

1A PREDICT, page 43

Answers will vary. Possible answers:

1. He is drawing on the wall.
2. He is in a building / in the subway / somewhere cold (he has a jacket on).
3. *Answers will vary.*

1B SHARE INFORMATION, page 44

Answers will vary. Suggested answers:

	Picture 1	Picture 2
1. What do you see in each picture?	the colors green and orange, a person, the number 84, a heart, a brain, movement, one arm goes through the head, one arm goes through the stomach, the person has no face or other details	the colors blue, red, and black; a person or baby on hands and knees ("on all fours"); black lines are around the person like the rays of the sun.
2. Give each picture a name or title.	*Answers will vary.*	*Answers will vary.*
3. Which picture is more interesting to you?	*Answers will vary.*	*Answers will vary.*

1C BACKGROUND AND VOCABULARY

2, pages 46–47

2. famous
3. museums
4. ads
5. public
6. drawing
7. painting
8. sculpture
9. graffiti

2A READING ONE

1, pages 47–48

Answers will vary. Suggested answers:

People	Places	Things	Ideas / Activities
children police	Kutztown, PA School of Visual Arts Europe Asia USA NYC Tokyo Shafrazi Gallery the Pop Shop	art graffiti art shows	helping people making art

READ FOR MAIN IDEAS, page 49

1. a   2. b   3. a

READ FOR DETAILS, page 50

1. energy
2. graffiti
3. public
4. ads
5. decide
6. Social issues
7. money

2B READING TWO

2, page 51

1. Some   2. snake   3. posters

STEP 1: Organize, page 52

Answers will vary. Suggested answers:

Ideas in Haring's Art	Untitled, 1984	Radiant Baby	Stop Aids	Free South Africa
Politics	✓		✓	✓
AIDS			✓	
Love	✓	✓		
Energy	✓	✓	✓	✓
Freedom				✓
Children		✓		
Other: ___				

STEP 2: Synthesize, page 52

Answer will vary. Suggested answers:

1. *Radiant Baby* is about <u>children</u> and hope for the future. There are rays around the child—like the rays of the sun. This shows the <u>energy</u> of the child.
2. *Stop AIDS* shows how people can work together to end a serious problem such as <u>AIDS</u>.
3. *Free South Africa* is about <u>politics</u>. This picture is about the fight for <u>freedom</u>.
4. In *Untitled, 1984*, you see a person. The person's arms go through his heart and brain. This picture shows how <u>love</u> is difficult.

REVIEW, page 53

Across

6. Art   10. Social
8. pop   11. energy
9. graffiti   12. ads

Down

3. famous   7. painter
4. drawings   9. galleries
5. different

EXPAND

2, pages 55–56

1. dance, dancer, dancing
2. drawing, draw, drawing
3. energy, energize, energetic
4. free, freedom
5. paint, painting, Painting, painter
6. politics, political

7. The public, publicize, public
8. sculptor, Sculpting, sculpture

3B GRAMMAR

1, page 57

AW: <u>Was</u> Haring different from other artists?

ER: Yes, he <u>was</u>.

AW: How <u>was</u> he different?

ER: Haring liked to make art in public places, like in the subway. He believed "art is for everyone." First, he <u>was</u> famous for his public art. Later, he became famous in galleries and museums.

He <u>was</u> also different because magazines <u>had</u> ads with his paintings and drawings. His drawings <u>were</u> also on other things, such as Swatch watches. He also sold his art in the Pop Shop. He used his art in unusual ways to communicate with the world.

was 5   *were* 1   *had* 1

When do we use *am, is, are,* and *have*? Present tense

When do we use *was, were,* and *had*? Past tense

2, page 59

2. were, were	7. was	12. was, wasn't
3. weren't, was	8. didn't have	13. were
4. had	9. was	14. was
5. was	10. was	15. was
6. had	11. was	16. didn't have

3, page 60

2. Was Haring famous in the 1970s?
3. Was Keith Haring energetic?
4. In what city was Haring born?
5. Was Haring only a painter?
6. Why was his art controversial?
7. Was the Pop Shop a restaurant?
8. Where were the two Pop Shops?
9. How old was Keith Haring in 1990?

4, page 60

Answers will vary. Suggested answers:

2. No, he wasn't. He was famous in the 1980s.
3. Yes, he was. He worked a lot.
4. He was born in Kutztown, PA.
5. No, he wasn't. He was also a sculptor.
6. It was controversial because sometimes it was about politics and relationships.
7. No, it wasn't. It was a store.
8. They were in New York and Tokyo.
9. He was 32 in 1990.

PREPARE TO WRITE

1, page 61

Answers may vary slightly. Suggested answers:

2. Keith Haring was born on May 4, 1958.
3. Haring was arrested in 1981 for drawing in the subway.
4. Haring was an art student in 1978 and 1979 at the School of Visual Arts in New York City.
5. His first drawings were graffiti in the New York City subway system.
6. His first important show was in 1982 at the Tony Shafrazi Gallery in New York City.

WRITE

1, page 62

a. 2   e. 1
b. 6   f. 3
c. 7   g. 4
d. 5

3, page 62

1, 2, 5, 3, 4, 6

REVISE

2, page 63

1. Haring was born on May 4, 1958.
2. Haring moved to New York, New York, in 1978.
3. He had his first important show in 1982.
4. Haring opened the Pop Shop in New York City in 1986. It closed in September of 1995.
5. The Pop Shop in Tokyo, Japan, opened on January 30, 1988. It closed in 1989.
6. Keith Haring was in Pisa, Italy, on Sunday, June 19, 1989.
7. Haring died on Friday, February 16, 1990.

UNIT 4

1A PREDICT, page 65

Answers will vary. Suggested answers:

1. He has a watch.
2. The watch was made in 1932. It is valuable. Where did you get it?
3. He is happy about the watch. He is thinking about his (grand)father.

1C BACKGROUND AND VOCABULARY, pages 66–67

1. experts   5. rare
2. guests   6. items
3. sentimental   7. condition
4. educational   8. valuable

READ FOR MAIN IDEAS, page 69

1. T (para. 3)   3. F (para. 4)
2. F (para. 4)   4. F (para. 5)

READ FOR DETAILS, page 69

1. e (2)   4. d (5)
2. c (3)   5. b (6)
3. a (5)   6. f (7)

MAKE INFERENCES, page 69

1. F   3. T
2. F   4. T

2B READING TWO

2, page 71

a. Rule 2   c. Rule 1
b. Rule 4   d. Rule 3

STEP 1: Organize, page 71

Answers will vary. Suggested answers:

	Ideas from Dan Stone's letter
Rule 1: Enjoy	Dan doesn't like baseball, but his collection has sentimental value.
Rule 2: Learn	He watches *Antiques Roadshow*.
Rule 3: Look for the best	His baseball cards are in perfect condition.
Rule 4: Buy rare items	The baseball is rare. It was signed by two famous baseball players.

REVIEW, page 72

1. valuable, condition
2. antique, worth
3. collect, collection, collector
4. rare, sentimental
5. history, favorite, expert

EXPAND, page 73

NOUNS: collection, collector, condition, education, excitement, expert, possession, sports, value

ADJECTIVES: collectible, educational, excited, exciting, expert, sentimental, sports, valuable

VERBS: collect, educate, excite, value

3B GRAMMAR

1, page 74

1. Ten (*am, love, love, have, watch, rings, don't answer, tell, am watching,* and *isn't*)
2. *don't answer* and *isn't*
3. the present

2, page 75

2. have
3. remember
4. wear
5. Do (you) wear
6. do
7. take
8. do (you) know
9. don't know
10. doesn't think
11. is
12. Does (it) look
13. is
14. isn't
15. is
16. love
17. plan
18. want
19. has

WRITE

1, page 77

1. Antiques experts like to be on *Antiques Roadshow* because it is good for their business.
2. The writer continues on the same line.
3. The writer stops at the end of the right margin.

2, page 78

Paragraph 1

    One day, a man named Russ Pritchard was a guest on *Antiques Roadshow*. He had a large sword. When he was young, Pritchard found the sword in his new house. George Juno, an antiques expert, told Pritchard it was an American Civil War sword. Juno said the sword was very rare and worth $35,000. Pritchard was very surprised to hear this.

Paragraph 2

    Two years later, there was a story in the newspaper about Pritchard and Juno. WGBH, a Boston TV station, learned that Pritchard's story was not true. Pritchard and Juno made up the story together. WGBH was very angry because it wants only true stories on *Antiques Roadshow*. As a result, Juno cannot be on *Antiques Roadshow* in the future.

3, page 79

One of my special possessions is my collection of family photographs.

4, page 79

(b.) My high school soccer shirt is very important to me.

REVISE

1, page 80

    My bicycle is a very special possession. My bike is not worth a lot of money. It is old, but it is in good condition. I ride my bike every day. I ride it to school, to the store, and to my grandmother's house. ~~I walk to these places in the summer.~~ I can go wherever I want because I have a bike.

UNIT 5

1A PREDICT, page 83

Answer will vary. Suggested answers:

1. They are members of a club / a gang / the military or army / the Guardian Angels.
2. They are wearing jackets / T-shirts (with a logo) / hats or berets (with pins on them) / uniforms.
3. They have meetings / make trouble / fight crime.
4. together stronger / When people work together, they are stronger / can do a lot.

1C BACKGROUND AND VOCABULARY

2, page 85

2. g   4. c   6. h   8. d
3. f   5. a   7. c

2A READING ONE

1, page 86

2. Start smoking
3. Arrested for drugs
4. Arrested for violent crimes
5. Hurt by guns
6. Killed by guns

READ FOR MAIN IDEAS, page 88

The Urban Angels program . . .

2. helps its members feel good about themselves.
4. teaches its members about social issues.
5. teaches young people about community service.

READ FOR DETAILS, page 89

1. c   3. f   5. b   7. a
2. d   4. h   6. g   8. e

2B READING TWO

2, page 91

1. b   2. b   3. a

STEP 1: Organize, page 91

Urban Angels Teaches At-Risk Teenagers to . . .	Kathy . . .	Melissa . . .
avoid drugs, gangs, guns, and crime	doesn't smoke or take drugs	won't join a gang
stay in school	wants to stay in school to become a fashion designer	gets good grades
be positive members of the community / be role models	wants to live in the neighborhood when she is an adult	teaches her sister about drugs and crime, helps her with her homework

2. teenagers
3. at-risk
4. avoid
5. crime
6. join
7. grades
8. role models
9. respect
10. members
11. positive
12. support

EXPAND, page 94

2, page 94

Conversation 1: fall through the cracks

Conversation 2: set a bad example

Conversation 3: give / lend me a hand

Conversation 4: reach out to

3B GRAMMAR

1, page 96

1. they
2. them
3. their

2, page 97

2. He, his
3. he, he
4. him
5. he, he
6. him, his
7. he
8. He
9. him
10. He
11. he, his, him
12. He

3, page 98

2. her
3. her
4. She
5. She
6. her
7. her
8. They
9. her
10. he
11. he
12. her
13. Her
14. she
15. her
16. she
17. them

WRITE

2, page 102

1. Maude Moran is a high school art teacher.
2. She is writing about the Neighborhood Arts Center.
3. She supports the Neighborhood Arts Center because it teaches people about art and helps local artists.

REVISE

1, page 103

Students underline these sentences on page 101:

Urban Angels help teens avoid problems such as drugs, crime, and gangs.

For example, they paint over graffiti at neighborhood "paint-outs."

2, page 103

1. The Neighborhood Arts Center helps children. For example, children can learn about art.
2. The Neighborhood Arts Center has many art classes such as painting, drawing, and sculpture.
3. The Neighborhood Arts Center has classes for all ages, such as children, college students, adults, and senior citizens.
4. The art classes are not expensive. For example, a drawing class costs $15 per semester.
5. The Neighborhood Arts Center supports local artists, For example, they teach classes at the Arts Center.
6. The gift shop sells art by local artists, such as jewelry, paintings, and pottery

UNIT 6

1A PREDICT, page 107

Answers will vary. Suggested answers:

1. It is closed. There are three signs: "closed," "out of business," and "for sale."
2. "Out of business" means that the company had problems and had to close permanently.
3. *Answers will vary.*

1C BACKGROUND AND VOCABULARY

1, page 109

1. d
2. e
3. g
4. b
5. f
6. a
7. c

2, page 109

Answers will vary. Suggested answers:

2. My father went to the hardware store to buy tools.
3. If Bob needs aspirin, he gets it at the drugstore.
4. Let's go to the video store. I want to rent a movie at home tonight.
5. Lisa gets her pens and paper for school at the office supply store in the mall.
6. You can buy a computer online or go to an electronics store.
7. Jack gets his hair cut at the barbershop on Main Street.

4, page 110

a. benefits
b. discount
c. owner
d. loyal
e. customers
f. compete
g. employees
h. selection

READ FOR MAIN IDEAS, page 113

2. a   3. b   4. a

READ FOR DETAILS, pages 113–114

2. a   5. d
3. c   6. a
4. c   7. b

2B READING TWO

2, page 115

1. 8,500   3. 60,000
2. 5,000   4. 1.5 million

STEP 1: Organize, page 116

Answers will vary. Suggested answers:

	Advantages	**Disadvantages**
Captain Video	• Employees know a lot about movies • Offers discounts • Has longer rental times	• Needs customer support • Has to increase prices because of competition
Blockbuster	• Many locations • Online service	• No "mom and pop" store feeling

REVIEW, pages 117–118

2. owner   7. discounts
3. customers   8. loyal
4. benefit   9. employees
5. coupons   10. enjoyed
6. selection   11. compete

EXPAND, pages 119–120

1. competitors, compete, competition, competitive
2. employs, employees, employed
3. benefits, benefited, beneficial
4. loyal, loyalty
5. owns, owner, own
6. serves, serve, service

3B GRAMMAR

1, page 121

1. *there is*: 2, *there isn't*: 1, *there are*: 3, *there aren't*: 1
2. *there is*: a McDonald's, a (flower) shop
   there isn't: noise
3. *there are*: students and professors, businesses, (video) stores
   there aren't: (chain) stores

2, page 123

1. are   6. are
2. are   7. was
3. are   8. is
4. wasn't   9. is
5. are   10. Is

PREPARE TO WRITE

2, page 125

1. It's a restaurant.
2. *Answers will vary.* It's next to the post office. It's across from the department store. It's next to the bank on Main Street.

WRITE

1, page 126

1. A restaurant that serves salads.
2. It's on Main Street, next to the post office and across from the department store.
3. It sells bread, salads, and soup(s).
4. It is bright and cheerful.
5. It is a great place to eat.

2, page 126

fresh   bright
large   cheerful
tasty   great
big

3, pages 126–127

2. big   5. friendly
3. comfortable   6. near my house
4. next to the window

REVISE

1, page 128

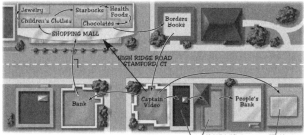

2, page 128

2. next to
3. between
4. around the corner from
5. across from
6. in front of
7. to the right of

UNIT 7

1A PREDICT, page 131

Answers will vary. Suggested answers:

1. It's a small airplane.
2. It is old (because of the propeller / the controls).
3. *Answers will vary.*

1B SHARE INFORMATION

1, page 132

1. Richard Nixon
2. Marilyn Monroe
3. Nelson Mandela
4. Christopher Reeve
5. Vincent van Gogh
6. Pu Yi
7. Diana Spencer

1C BACKGROUND AND VOCABULARY, page 133

2. pilot
3. took off
4. contest
5. landed
6. set a record
7. flight
8. hero
9. media

READ FOR MAIN IDEAS, pages 135–136

1. b   2. b   3. a   4. c

READ FOR DETAILS, pages 136–137

Answers will vary. Suggested answers:

2. Lindbergh took off from New York on the 20th (of May).
3. He took off at 7:52 A.M.
4. There was only one person on the plane.
5. His flight was 3,610 miles (long).
6. He was in the air for 33½ hours.
7. He brought five sandwiches with him.
8. He landed in Paris on the 21st (of May).
9. About 150,000 people greeted him when he arrived in Paris.

2B READING TWO

2, page 138

Answers will vary. Suggested answers:

He was an international hero.
He was a contest winner.
He was an author.
He was a Pulitzer Prize winner.

He was *Time* magazine's "Man of the Year."
He was a father.
He was an inventor.
He was an enemy to some people.
He was an environmentalist.

STEP 1: Organize, page 139

Answers will vary. Suggested answers:

High Points	Low Points
He flew non-stop and solo from New York to Paris.	Some people called him "anti-American" and "a Nazi."
He visited presidents, kings, and queens.	He moved his family to England to protect them from the media.
He received $25,000 for winning the contest.	He died of cancer.
He traveled around the world.	
He was "Man of the Year."	
He married Anne Morrow.	
He had children.	
He won a Pulitzer Prize.	
He invented an artificial heart.	

REVIEW, page 140

2. flew
3. flight
4. hero
5. called
6. set
7. took off
8. landed
9. fly
10. media

EXPAND, page 141

2. landed
3. solo
4. handsome
5. contest
6. media
7. famous
8. flight
9. pilot

3B GRAMMAR

1, page 142

1. kidnapped, asked, arrested, died
2. left, paid, found, was, said
3. Use *did* + *not* + base form of the verb.

2, page 144

2. wanted
3. wanted
4. tried
5. was
6. was
7. died
8. did
9. arrived
10. called
11. became
12. was
13. did not change
14. had
15. was not
16. did not want
17. thought
18. was
19. did not agree
20. did not think
21. was

WRITE

1, page 146

6, 7, 8, 1, 4, 5, 3, 2

2, page 147

My husband and I had a wonderful honeymoon trip four years ago. First, we flew to New York City on Monday. The next day, we went to the Metropolitan Museum of Art and the Statue of Liberty. On Wednesday, we rented a car and drove to Vermont. We went swimming and hiking, and we relaxed. Then we drove to New York City on Sunday morning. Finally, we flew home on Sunday night. It was a great vacation.

3, page 147

(✓) Five years ago, my friend and I had a terrible vacation in Florida. Everything went wrong. First, we almost missed our plane. Then we lost our luggage. We arrived in Florida with no clothes, so we went shopping for new clothes. Next, it rained for two days. Finally, it stopped raining, and we went to the beach. Then we went home the next day. It was a terrible vacation.

REVISE

1, page 148

Five years ago, First, Then, Next, Finally, Then, the next day

2, page 149

2. The next day
3. for about six hours
4. Finally

UNIT 8

IC BACKGROUND AND VOCABULARY

1, page 153

1. committee
2. solutions
3. convenient
4. heavy traffic
5. commute
6. on time
7. meeting

3, page 154

helicopter	highway
tunnel	lanes
train	subway

READ FOR MAIN IDEAS, page 156

2

READ FOR DETAILS, page 157

2. d   4. h   6. a   8. g
3. c   5. i   7. f   9. b

2B READING TWO

2, page 159

1. T   2. T

STEP I: Organize, page 160

Answers will vary. Suggested answers:

Trucks: tunnel under city
Poor condition of roads and bridges: traffic tax
Streets not safe for pedestrians: sky train, helicopter
Streets not safe for bicyclists: bike lanes
Slow buses: sky train, helicopter
Pollution, including noise: tunnel under city, sky train, Deduct-a-Ride

REVIEW, page 161

2. Heavy traffic   7. convenient
3. commute   8. committee
4. on time   9. solutions
5. meetings   10. Pedestrians
6. subway

EXPAND, page 162

1, page 162

1. takes   5. takes   9. go
2. get   6. take   10. takes
3. takes   7. take   11. go
4. take   8. get

3B GRAMMAR

1, page 164

b. 2   c. 3   d. 2   e. 1

2, page 165

Answers may vary. Suggested answers:

2. The New York City subway is busier.
3. The London Underground is more expensive to ride.
4. The New York City subway is probably noisier.
5. The London Underground is older.

WRITE

2, page 168

Topic sentence (**main idea**): Walking is better than driving.
    Reason 1: Walking is usually faster.
    Explanation: Traffic is heavy and moves slowly.
    Reason 2: Walking is more enjoyable. I can relax when I walk.
    Explanation: I get upset when the traffic is slow.
    Reason 3: I get exercise when I walk.
    Explanation: My office is one mile away. I don't get exercise if I drive.

REVISE

1, page 169

Students underline:

One reason is that, Another reason is that, The most important reason is that

UNIT 9

1C BACKGROUND AND VOCABULARY, page 173

1. b   **3.** a   **5.** a   **7.** b

2. a   **4.** b   **6.** a

2A READING ONE, page 174

1. 4,058,814   **4.** 132,219

2. 128,717   **5.** 6208

3. 468   **6.** The number is going up.

READ FOR MAIN IDEAS, page 176

1. T   **2.** F   **3.** T   **4.** F

READ FOR DETAILS, page 177

1. one   **7.** six

2. 3,407   **8.** 15

3. two   **9.** five

4. Forty   **10.** 150, 170

5. four, four   **11.** five, five

6. four, three   **12.** Two

MAKE INFERENCES, page 177

Answers will vary. Suggested answers:

- Yes, they have a strong marriage. They make important decisions together. They both love children. They have a "date night" every Friday.
- No, they don't have a strong marriage. They are too busy and tired.

2B READING TWO

2, page 179

1. F   **2.** T   **3.** ?   **4.** T

STEP 1: Organize, page 180

Answers will vary. Suggested answers:

Having a Big Family		
	Pros	**Cons**
The McCaugheys	• many different personalities • support • laughter	• noisy • a lot of work
The Dionnes	• support (later in life)	• no privacy • no love from family • people want to make money • too much attention

REVIEW, page 182

2. jealous   **7.** entertainment

3. laughter   **8.** unique

4. protect   **9.** siblings

5. challenge   **10.** donate

6. privacy

EXPAND, pages 183–184

1. the black sheep   **5.** raise a family

2. takes after   **6.** the middle child

3. runs in the (Sullivan) family   **7.** an only child

4. sibling rivalry   **8.** grow up

3B GRAMMAR

1, page 184

1. He should give Cole an allowance, but he shouldn't give him too much. He should give him just enough for small things. He should teach Cole to save money "for a rainy day."

2. The base form

2, pages 185–186

2. Should my teenage son; should

3. How many hours a day should I let; shouldn't; should

4. Should parents let; should; should

5. Should we make; shouldn't; should

6. Should children always follow; shouldn't; should

7. Should parents require; should; should

8. Should adult children move out; should

PREPARE TO WRITE

1, pages 188–189

Answers will vary. Suggested answers:

2. Why do you think that? / How many brothers and sisters did you have? / Were there three kids in your family?

3. Why do you say that? / Why four or five years?

4. Why do you say that? / Didn't you get along well with your brothers and sisters?

WRITE

1, page 190

1. Families should have only one child.
2. **a.** Children are expensive.
   b. Parents are busy. They can't give enough attention to more than one child.

REVISE

1, page 191

b

2, page 191

1. c, repetition   2. b, opinion   3. a, the future

UNIT 10

1A PREDICT, page 193

Answers will vary. Suggested answers:

There's a girl / young woman. She's dreaming about playing soccer. She's thinking about being a professional player. She's imagining doing a TV interview.

1C BACKGROUND AND VOCABULARY

2, page 195

2. d	5. b	8. g
3. i	6. c	9. f
4. a	7. e	

READ FOR MAIN IDEAS, page 197

3

READ FOR DETAILS, page 198

1. c   2. c   3. b   4. a   5. c

MAKE INFERENCES, page 198

1. d	3. e	5. b
2. a	4. c	6. f

2B READING TWO

2, page 201

1. T   2. T   3. F   4. T   5. T

STEP 1: Organize, page 201

Answers will vary. Suggested answers:

		Freddy Adu	Bram Tarek
1.	What is he learning before he joins the professional world?	• Adu is learning how to live in the spotlight. • He is learning to be responsible.	• Tarek is learning that family, education, and health are more important than money. • He wants to learn about working with other people (to be a leader).
2.	Where or how is he learning these lessons?	• In school and from older players	• By talking to other players and staying in school
3.	What are some difficulties that young pro players might have?	• Dealing with comments made by the media • Not being mature enough • People wanting your money	• Young athletes think money is the most important thing.

REVIEW, page 203

2. a good job
3. She talks to her boyfriend on the phone while she babysits.
4. the supermarket
5. forgets
6. walking
7. do my homework
8. He was a good dancer.
9. He made millions of dollars.
10. He played basketball every day.

EXPAND

2, page 205

1. b   2. d   3. a   4. c   5. e

3B GRAMMAR

1, page 208

1. b	3. a	5. b	7. a
2. a	4. b	6. b	

2, page 210

1. Kareem Abdul-Jabbar is too old to play pro basketball.
2. Joe is a very talented musician.
3. Kevin is tall enough to play basketball.
4. Jamie is not old enough to drive.
5. Sally is not strong enough to pick up the box.
6. Martina was good enough to win at Wimbledon.

3, pages 210–211

Answers may vary.

2. Jeff is too young to ride The Sled.
3. Jeff isn't heavy enough to ride The Sled.
4. Charlie is tall enough to ride The Sled.
5. Charlie is heavy enough to ride The Sled.
6. Charlie is old enough to ride The Sled.
7. Ayala is too tall to ride The Sled.
8. Ayala is too old to ride The Sled.

WRITE

2, page 213

Answers may vary.

8 This is a good idea if you want to get an athletic scholarship to pay for college.
4 I think you should choose one sport.
2 I played sports when I was in high school, too.
5 If you do this, you will have more time for school work.
1 I understand your situation.
6 You will also need enough time to sleep. Your body needs time to rest.
10 Colleges will also notice your grades.
11 I'm sure you will make the right decision.
12 Good luck.
3 I was often too tired at night to finish my homework or even eat dinner!
7 If you focus on one sport, you will get better at it. Colleges will notice.
9 You'll also have more time for homework

REVISE

1, page 216

Answers will vary. Suggested answers:

1. You should look for a job. / You shouldn't quit your job before you find a new one.
2. You ought to take one this year. / You had better take one or you will get sick.
3. You should find a hobby. / You might take up golf or do volunteer work.
4. You could get a part-time job. / You should cook more instead of eating out.
5. You should spend time on weekends with your family.
6. You shouldn't work so much.

7. You should get up earlier so you are not late.
8. You should tell your boss that you need to spend time with your family.
9. You can ask for a bigger office. / You might ask for a bigger office. / You could work in a large conference room.
10. You should see a doctor. You ought to take a vacation.
11. You should look for a more exciting job.
12. You should ask for your own desk.

Unit Word List

The **Unit Word List** is a summary of key vocabulary from the student book. The words are presented by unit, in alphabetical order.

UNIT 1

advice
chat
community
goal
laugh
meet
peace
personal
quote (noun)
safe
user
volunteer

Expressions:

It's nice to meet you.
It was nice to meet you.
Nice chatting with you.
Nice meeting you again.
Nice talking to you.
Nice to meet you (again).
Nice to see you again.

UNIT 2

clothes
comfortable
decrease (verb)
designer
expensive
fashion
increase (verb)
individuality
messy
neat
spirit
team
wear

Related verb phrases:

get dressed
put on

UNIT 3

ad
different
drawing
energetic
famous
gallery
graffiti
museum
painting
pop
public (adjective)
sculpture
shop
social (adjective)

Word forms:

dance, dancer, dancing
draw, drawing
energy, energetic,
    energize
freedom, free
paint, painting, painter
politics, politician,
    political
publicize, (the) public
sculpture, sculptor,
    sculpting, sculpt

UNIT 4

antique
collect
condition
educational
expert
favorite
guest
history
item
possession
rare
sentimental
valuable
worth (adjective)

Word forms:

collect, collectible,
    collection, collector
condition
educate, education,
    educational
excite, excited,
    excitement, exciting
value, valuable

UNIT 5

at-risk
avoid
crime
grade
join
member
positive
respect
role model
support (verb)
teenager
urban

Related verb phrases:

fall through the cracks
give / lend a hand
reach out to
set a good / bad example

UNIT 6

barbershop
benefit (noun)
bookstore
compete
coupon
customer
discount
drugstore
electronics store
employee
enjoy
hardware store
loyal
office supply store
owner
selection
video store

Word forms:

benefit, beneficial
compete, competitor,
    competition,
    competitive
employ, employed,
    employee
loyal, loyalty
own, owner
serve, service

UNIT 7

call (verb)
contest
flew
flight
fly
handsome
hero
land (verb)
married
media
pilot
plane
set a record
take off
writer

Synonyms:

arrived / landed
built / constructed
contest / competition
famous / well known
flight / trip
handsome / good looking
media / press
pilot / flier
price / cost
solo / alone
take off / depart

UNIT 8

committee
commute (verb)
convenient
heavy traffic
helicopter
highway
lane
meeting
on time
pedestrian
resident
solution
subway
train
tunnel

Related verbs:

get
go
take

UNIT 9

challenge (noun)
donate
entertainment
jealous
laughter
pregnant
privacy
protect
sibling
unique

Expressions:

an only child
grow up
It runs in the family.
raise children / a family
sibling rivalry
take after
the middle child

UNIT 10

coach
comment (noun)
deal with
difficulty
earn
graduate
hero
mature
responsible
talent

Expressions:

be a team player
be / get on the ball
call the shots
get the ball rolling
hog the (ball)

Achievement Tests
Unit 1

PART 1: READING

1.1 *Read part of an article about language learning. Check (✔) the best prediction of what the reading is about. There is only one right answer.*

If you want to practice a language with an international friend, join Europa Pages (www.europa-pages.com). It's free. You can build a community of friends from around the world and achieve your language goals.

_____ **A.** a magazine

_____ **B.** an international show

_____ **C.** a website

_____ **D.** an online game

1.2 *Now read the entire article. Use the information to choose the correct answers.*

Join Europa Pages

Do you want language learning to be more fun? Students at Wilson High School have fun studying foreign languages. They chat with pen pals from other countries.

Welcome to Europa Pages (www.europa-pages.com), the website about language and friendship. If you want to practice a language with an international friend, join Europa Pages. It's free. You can build a community of friends from around the world and achieve your language goals.

Keyana Campbell, a sophomore, has a pen pal in Granada, Spain. Keyana said, "I chat with Rosa, my pen pal, every week online. I practice Spanish, and she practices English. We laugh and have a lot of fun."

Mitch Jacobs, a freshman, is learning French. His pen pal, Jacques, lives in Paris, France. "Jacques helps me with my French. He gives me advice that helps me to remember vocabulary," Mitch said.

Senior Debbie Sanchez has a pen pal, Luis, in Argentina. "We practice a lot. We e-mail each other every day. Writing is easier than talking on the phone or face to face. I don't get nervous when I write."

Europa Pages is safe. Some of the people at Europa Pages are volunteers. They work there because they love the website. They make sure the website is safe for everyone. Europa Pages never asks users to enter personal information such as their address or credit card number.

Europa Pages has two goals: to help people learn foreign languages and to help people make friends worldwide. When people make international friends, they bring more peace to the world.

Check (✔) the best answer to complete each sentence.

1. Students at Wilson High School join Europa Pages to _____.

   _____ **A.** do homework   _____ **C.** give advice

   _____ **B.** get credit cards   _____ **D.** study languages

2. Students who visit Europa Pages are probably _____.

   _____ **A.** friendly   _____ **C.** nervous

   _____ **B.** funny   _____ **D.** unfriendly

1.3 *Check (✔) the four words that were used to describe Europa Pages.*

   _____ **A.** easy   _____ **D.** new

   _____ **B.** free   _____ **E.** quick

   _____ **C.** fun   _____ **F.** safe

1.4 *Read the passage from "Welcome to MySpace" in* NorthStar: Reading and Writing 1, *Unit 1. Use the information from this reading and "Join Europa Pages" to complete the activity. The first one has been done for you.*

Welcome to MySpace

MySpace is friendly and easy to use. MySpace users can make personal webpages. . . . MySpace users can visit your personal webpage and chat with you.

Some people say that there are two problems. First, there is no one to watch MySpace carefully to make it safe for everyone. Second, other Internet companies can copy your personal information and pictures. Your personal information can stay on the Internet long after you stop using MySpace. But MySpace is still very popular.

	MySpace	Europa Pages	Both
Very popular	✓		
1. Fun			
2. Has language practice			
3. Not safe			

PART 2: VOCABULARY

2.1 *Read the letter. Use the words from the box to fill in the blanks. Do not use words more than once. Not all of the words will be used.*

advice	community	laugh	peace	quote	screen
chat	goals	meet	personal	safe	volunteers

Hi Tim,

Thank you for asking about Europa Pages.

Europa Pages is a great place to _____ other people. The website has
                                                    1.

different rooms for people to _____ with each other. We are like a
                                                2.

big _____ of friends! Take my _____—you should go to
            3.   **4.**

Europa Pages. There is no danger, so it's very _____. Several
                                                                        5.

_____ help to keep it safe. They bring _____ to the website.
        6.   **7.**

    Europa Pages keeps your _____ information safe, too. I know one
                                            8.

of your _____ is to learn a language. So, visit the website, have fun,
                9.

and _____ with everyone. The website is www.europa-pages.com.
            10.

See you there!

Your friends at Europa Pages

PART 3: SKILLS FOR WRITING

3.1 *Read the paragraph. Then answer the questions.*

Europa Pages is safe. Some of the people at Europa Pages are volunteers. They work there because they love the website. they make sure, the website is safe for everyone. Europa Pages never asks users to enter personal information, such as their address or credit card number.

1. What is the subject of the first sentence?

   _____

2. How many verbs are in the second sentence?

   _____

3. What is the verb in the second sentence?

   _____

4. Which sentence has a capitalization error?

   _____

5. Which sentence has incorrect punctuation?

   _____

3.2 *Write questions using* **be** *or* **have**.

1. Who / have / to pay / for Europa Pages?

   _____

2. Keyana Campbell / be / learning / Spanish?

   _____

3. You / have / many friends / at Europa Pages?

   _____

4. The website / have / volunteers / to help?

   _____

5. Where / be / Jacques and Debbie / from?

   _____

PART 4: WRITING

A Descriptive Paragraph (20 minutes)

Write a paragraph about a website that you use.
- Describe the website and tell why you like it.
- Use complete sentences.
- Organize your paragraph by ideas.
- Use the vocabulary and grammar from Unit 1.

Unit 1 Vocabulary Words				
advice	community	friendly	peace	safe
chat	face to face	laugh	personal	volunteers

Unit 1 Grammar: Questions with *Be* and *Have*
• Who *is* that person? • What does he *have*?

Achievement Tests
Unit 2

PART 1: READING

1.1 *Read the beginning of a letter. Check (✔) the best prediction of what the reading is about. There is only one right answer.*

Dear Abby,

Last week the principal of my daughter's high school sent a letter to all parents. The letter said that students will wear uniforms beginning next year. I am very concerned about this. Uniforms are a terrible idea.

_____ **A.** a high school principal   _____ **C.** school uniforms

_____ **B.** a high school student   _____ **D.** next year's classes

1.2 *Now read the entire letter and Abby's response. Use the information to choose the correct answers.*

A Letter to Abby

Dear Abby,

Last week the principal of my daughter's high school sent a letter to all parents. The letter said that students will wear uniforms beginning next year. I am very concerned about this. Uniforms are a terrible idea.

A uniform will be more expensive than the regular clothes my daughter puts on every day. I have three other children. I cannot afford to spend any more money on their clothes. My daughter is upset, too. She says, "Mom, a uniform will decrease my individuality. You know I have my own taste in fashion. And I like clothes that are comfortable. A *dress* is not comfortable."

Please tell me, Abby, what can I do?

Sincerely,
Susan Rosenstein

Dear Susan,

I understand your concern. It is true that some uniforms are expensive, but most uniforms are cheaper than designer clothes. Also, your daughter will wear the same uniform every day. This means that you will not need to buy a lot of other clothes. Although your child will dress like the other students, this is positive for many reasons. It will not matter if a student's family is rich or poor. All students will feel equal because they all will wear the same uniforms. Furthermore, it will be easy for them to get dressed every day. They will not have to spend time choosing clothes to wear. Parents will know that their children will look neat, not messy. In addition, school uniforms increase school spirit. Students will feel like they are part of a team. I hope this helps.

Sincerely,
Abby

Check (✔) the best answer to complete each sentence.

1. People probably write to Abby to get _____.

_____ **A.** advice

_____ **B.** clothes

_____ **C.** money

_____ **D.** spirit

2. Susan Rosenstein _____.

_____ **A.** does not care about school uniforms

_____ **B.** does not like the school principal

_____ **C.** does not think uniforms are comfortable

_____ **D.** does not want school uniforms

3. Abby thinks wearing uniforms is _____ for students.

_____ **A.** exciting

_____ **B.** expensive

_____ **C.** negative

_____ **D.** positive

1.3 *Write the three words or phrases from the box that Abby uses to talk about school uniforms.*

comfortable	feel equal	increase school spirit	neat
fashion	gray	look messy	regular

1. _____

2. _____

3. _____

1.4 *Read the passage from "A Letter From the Principal" in* NorthStar: Reading and Writing 1, *Unit 2. Use the information from this reading and "A Letter to Abby" to complete the activity. Write the letter of the statement under the name of the porson who believes it is true. Not all of the statements will be used. The first one has been done for you.*

A Letter from the Principal

Wearing a uniform is a good idea. The uniform will help students study hard. They will think about school and school work, not about fashion. Today, students think too much about clothes and how they look. It is important to think about education first.

Uniforms also look neat and clean. When students are neat and clean, they are more comfortable. When they are more comfortable, they study more.

Sincerely,
Peter F. Collins

A. ~~Students study more when they are comfortable.~~

B. Uniforms are expensive and not comfortable.

C. Sometimes students don't want to be neat.

D. School uniforms can help increase school spirit.

E. Students should think more about their education.

F. Students need to wear designer clothes to feel good.

Mr. Collins	Mrs. Rosenstein	Abby
1. A and	2.	3.

PART 2: VOCABULARY

2.1 *Check (✔) the best answer to complete each sentence.*

1. **Designer** clothes are _____.

   _____ A. inexpensive clothes

   _____ B. like colorful uniforms

   _____ C. made by a famous company

   _____ D. the same as all clothes

2. If something is **expensive**, it _____.

    ____ **A.** has a high price

    ____ **B.** is comfortable

    ____ **C.** is cheap

    ____ **D.** is clean

3. When a price **decreases**, the price _____.

    ____ **A.** becomes less

    ____ **B.** becomes more

    ____ **C.** changes often

    ____ **D.** stays the same

4. To **get dressed** means to _____.

    ____ **A.** buy new clothes

    ____ **B.** clean your clothes

    ____ **C.** put clothes on

    ____ **D.** take clothes off

5. If something is **messy**, it is _____.

    ____ **A.** easy to wear

    ____ **B.** not neat

    ____ **C.** in order

    ____ **D.** popular

2.2 *Complete the sentences by unscrambling the boldfaced words.*

1. My high school makes students put on **sfinuorm.** _____

2. The school thinks that uniforms will make everyone **laque.**
   _____

3. Students should decide what clothes they want to **wrae.** _____

4. They should have clothes that are **lecmoorfbat.** _____

5. Students like different kinds of clothes. They should decide their own
   nfosiha. _____

PART 3: SKILLS FOR WRITING

3.1 *Match the two parts of each sentence. You will not use all of the answers. One answer is already given.*

_D_	Uniforms are a bad idea because	A. they make students feel like a team.
___ 1.	Some parents are not happy because	B. one student tore her uniform.
___ 2.	Uniforms help to increase school spirit because	C. their children have to wear uniforms.
___ 3.	Uniforms are a good idea because	D. ~~students will not be comfortable~~.
		E. all students must be on a team.
		F. parents know their children will look neat.

3.2 *Complete the sentences with the words in parentheses. Put the adjectives in the right order.*

She is wearing a ____neat blue cotton____ skirt. (cotton, neat, blue)

1. He is wearing _____ pants. (black, wool, comfortable)

2. Sometimes she wears a _____ jacket to school. (plaid, green, messy)

3.3 *Complete the sentences. Use **will**, **will not**, or **won't**. In some sentences, both **will not** and **won't** may be correct.*

1. The teams _____ wear their uniforms tomorrow. They don't have a game.

2. _____ you go to the game tomorrow? It should be a lot of fun.

3. No, I probably _____. I have too much homework to do.

4. Yeah, I _____ do my homework first. Then I'll go to the game.

5. I guess I _____ see you there. Maybe we can meet after the game.

PART 4: WRITING

A Letter with an Opinion (20 minutes)

Write a short letter with your opinion about wearing school uniforms in high school. Do you think wearing uniforms is a good or bad idea?

- Tell what you are writing your opinion about.
- Describe your opinion.
- Give reasons with *because*.
- Use letter format.
- Use the vocabulary and grammar from Unit 2.

Unit 2 Vocabulary Words			
decrease	expensive	increase	put on
designer	fashion	messy	spirit
equal	get dressed	neat	uniform
Unit 2 Grammar: The Future with *Will*			
• I ***will*** buy some clothes for the party.			

Achievement Tests
Unit 3

Name: _____

Date: _____

PART 1: READING

1.1 *Read the beginning of an article. Check (✔) the best prediction of what the reading is about. There is only one right answer.*

Paul Jackson Pollock was an American painter who lived from 1912 to 1956. He made paintings but not drawings or sculptures. Pollock had a unique[1] style. His art was very different from other paintings. Pollock spilled colored paint onto large canvases.

_____ **A.** canvas   _____ **C.** a sculptor

_____ **B.** a painter   _____ **D.** drawings

1.2 *Now read the entire article. Use the information to choose the correct answers.*

Paul Jackson Pollock

Paul Jackson Pollock was an American painter who lived from 1912 to 1956. He made paintings but not drawings or sculptures. Pollock had a unique style. His art was very different from other paintings. Pollock spilled colored paint onto large canvases. He thought that his paintings were energetic because of their bright colors and big designs. He often put a canvas on the floor, walked around it, and dripped[2] paint all over it. However, many people did not like Pollock's paintings. They said that his art looked like graffiti.

   In 1949, Pollock started to become more famous. *Life Magazine* published an article that asked, "Is he the greatest living painter in the United States?" This article was like an ad for Pollock's paintings, and Pollock became a part of pop culture. People started to consider Pollock's paintings as statements about social history and politics. They thought his paintings symbolized freedom. However, Pollock had a hard, sad life. He suffered from depression and had a drinking problem. When he was 44 years old, Pollock died in a car accident. People still remember Pollock. Today we can see his paintings in museums all over the world.

---

[1] **unique:** not like anything else
[2] **dripped:** caused to fall in drops little by little

Check (✔) the best answer to complete each sentence.

1. Paul Jackson Pollock's art was _____.

    _____ **A.** dark   _____ **C.** old

    _____ **B.** depressing   _____ **D.** unique

2. People called his art "graffiti" because it was _____.

    _____ **A.** colorful   _____ **C.** famous

    _____ **B.** different   _____ **D.** great

3. The _____ made his paintings bright.

    _____ **A.** canvases   _____ **C.** designs

    _____ **B.** colors   _____ **D.** styles

1.3 *Write the correct numbers to complete the sentences.*

1. Paul Jackson Pollock started to become famous in _____.

2. Paul Jackson Pollock was _____ years old when he died.

3. Paul Jackson Pollock died in the year _____.

1.4 *Read the information from "Art for Everyone" in* NorthStar: Reading and Writing 1, *Unit 3. Use the information from this reading and "Paul Jackson Pollock" to complete the activity. Not all of the words will be used.*

Art for Everyone

When people asked Keith Haring, "What is your art about?" he answered, "You decide." His art is funny, energetic, and sometimes angry. It is also political. His art is about education, freedom, and AIDS. These social issues were very important to Haring. . . . Later, he became famous in galleries and museums. He was also different because magazines had ads with his paintings and drawings.

| culture   freedom   magazines   museums   politics   sculptures |

1. Haring's and Pollock's artwork both symbolized _____.

2. Their artwork was published in _____.

3. Today, their work can be found in _____.

PART 2: VOCABULARY

2.1 *Use the words from the box to fill in the blanks. Not all of the words will be used.*

| ads   artists   energetic   graffiti   money   pop   public   social issues |

1. Pollock's artwork was _____ because of the big designs.

2. Keith Haring drew _____ on walls and buildings in New York.

3. Pollock's artwork became part of _____ culture in the U.S.

4. Many works of art are used for magazine _____.

5. Many people think Haring's and Pollock's works are about _____.

2.2 *Fill in the chart with the correct words.*

Nouns	Verbs	Adjectives
society	X	**4.**
1.	draw	X
2.	free	free
dancer	**3.**	X
fame	X	**5.**

PART 3: SKILLS FOR WRITING

3.1 *Read the sentences about Keith Haring. Number the sentences in time order. The first one is numbered zero.*

____ **A.** Haring's family lived in Kutztown, Pennsylvania, in the 1970s.

____ **B.** Haring died of AIDS on February 16, 1990.

_0_ **C.** Keith Haring was born on Monday, May 4, 1958.

____ **D.** In 1988, Haring opened a Pop Shop in Tokyo, Japan.

3.2 *Add commas to the sentences. One answer is already given.*

Haring visited Madrid, Spain.

1. Paul Jackson Pollock visited Los Angeles California.

2. Haring lived in New York New York for several years.

3.3 *Complete the sentences with* **was**, **wasn't**, **were**, **had**, *or* **didn't have**.

1. Keith Haring _____ just a painter.

2. Paul Jackson Pollock _____ a drinking problem.

3. Both Haring and Pollock _____ famous artists.

4. Pollock _____ a very long life.

5. Haring _____ very popular with children.

PART 4: WRITING

A Biography (20 minutes)

Write a paragraph about a famous artist or another famous person from your country.

- Describe the person.
- Put events in time order, including dates and places.
- Use the vocabulary and grammar from Unit 3.

Unit 3 Vocabulary Words			
ads	energetic	graffiti	pop
different	famous	museum	sculpture
drawings	freedom	paintings	social issues
Unit 3 Grammar: Simple Past of *Be* and *Have*			
• I *was* in the cafeteria. I *had* pasta and a salad.			

Achievement Tests
Unit 4

Name: _____

Date: _____

PART 1: READING

1.1 *Read the beginning of a story. Check (✔) the word that best completes the sentence. There is only one right answer.*

Every morning I read my local newspaper. I find out where the yard sales[1] are. I go around to all of the yard sales. I am a regular guest. Everyone at the yard sales knows me because I go to all of the sales, and I buy old and rare things.

The person in this story probably collects _____.

_____ **A.** antiques   _____ **C.** newspapers

_____ **B.** guests   _____ **D.** sales

1.2 *Now read the entire story. Use the information to choose the correct answers.*

Try a New Career

Is your job boring? Do you want to try something new? If your answer is "yes," read about my job as a professional antiques collector. You can be an antiques collector, too.

Every morning I read my local newspaper. I find out where the yard sales are. I go around to all of the yard sales. I am a regular guest. Everyone at the yard sales knows me because I go to all of the sales, and I buy old and rare things. I buy antiques like lamps, furniture, and jewelry. Even though they are old, they are in good condition. They do not look very old. They have to be in good condition to be worth a lot of money.

I bring the things that I buy to antique dealers. They are the experts. They know a lot about antiques. They examine the antiques and tell me how valuable they are. One time I brought in a ring that was worth $50,000. Another time I had a painting that was worth $100,000! These things do not have sentimental value because I buy them at yard sales. They are not my family's possessions, so I sell these antiques, and I make a lot of money.

Do you want to become an antiques collector? Call me at (555) 782-5580 to learn more.

_____
[1] **yard sale:** a sale of used possessions held on the front yard of the seller's home

Check (✔) the paragraph where you can find the information.

1. The author is a professional antiques collector.

   _____ **A.** Paragraph 1   _____ **C.** Paragraph 3

   _____ **B.** Paragraph 2   _____ **D.** Paragraph 4

2. You can make a lot of money selling antiques.

   _____ **A.** Paragraph 1   _____ **C.** Paragraph 3

   _____ **B.** Paragraph 2   _____ **D.** Paragraph 4

1.3 *Check (✔) the best answer to complete each sentence.*

1. _____ antiques are very valuable.

   _____ **A.** New   _____ **C.** Regular

   _____ **B.** Rare   _____ **D.** Painted

2. The author thinks collecting antiques is _____.

   _____ **A.** boring   _____ **C.** exciting

   _____ **B.** difficult   _____ **D.** sentimental

3. The author takes antiques to _____ to determine their value.

   _____ **A.** experts   _____ **C.** families

   _____ **B.** guests   _____ **D.** yard sales

4. The author had a painting worth _____.

   _____ **A.** $ 5,000   _____ **C.** $ 50,000

   _____ **B.** $ 10,000   _____ **D.** $ 100,000

1.4 *Read the passage from "My Secret" in* NorthStar: Reading and Writing 1, *Unit 4. Use the information from this reading and "Try a New Career" to complete the activity. The first one has been done for you.*

My Secret

Here is my secret: On Monday nights I watch *Antiques Roadshow*. It is a show about antiques and collections. It's great! . . . I want *Antiques Roadshow* to visit my city. I can't wait! I have a baseball signed by Babe Ruth and Jackie Robinson in the 1940s. It's in perfect condition. I also have a baseball card collection. I keep it in a box under my bed. The ball and the cards have sentimental value. My father gave them to me. But I don't really like to play or watch baseball. Maybe they are worth a lot of money!

	"My Secret"	"Try a New Career"	Both	Neither
Thinks antiques can be worth a lot of money			✓	
1. Collects things with sentimental value				
2. Collects things in good condition				
3. Buys rare items				

PART 2: VOCABULARY

2.1 *Put the words from the box into three groups: nouns, adjectives, or verbs. Not all of the words will be used.*

antiques	history	smart
educate	secretly	valuable

Nouns	Adjectives	Verb
1.	3.	5.
2.	4.	

2.2 *Use the words from the box to fill in the blanks. Not all of the words will be used.*

collector	experts	guests	sentimental
condition	favorite	items	worth

1. My baseball card collection has _____ value for me.

2. The cards are really old. I think they are _____ a lot of money.

3. They are in the same _____ as when I was a little boy.

4. I bought them from a card _____ in my hometown.

5. He told me they will be valuable _____ some day.

PART 3: SKILLS FOR WRITING

3.1 *Complete the conversation with the present tense form of the verbs in parentheses.*

BETHANY: Welcome to my yard sale. _____ you _____
                                              1.   **2. (need)**
          any help?

STEVE: Not yet. I _____ one question though.
                          3. (have)

BETHANY: Sure. What _____ it?
                          4. (be)

STEVE: Well, my wife _____ antiques. She _____ to
                              5. (collect)   **6. (want)**
          buy everything. Is that OK?

BETHANY: Wow! Of course it is.

3.2 *Read the paragraph. Then check the best answer to each question.*

(1) *Antiques Roadshow* is a popular television show. (2) The show travels to different cities. (3) The guests are regular people. (4) The show is not very funny. (5) They bring their special possessions to the show. (6) They tell stories and ask questions. (7) You can see similar shows in other countries around the world.

1. Which is the topic sentence of the paragraph?

    ____ **A.** 1   ____ **C.** 6

    ____ **B.** 2   ____ **D.** 7

2. Which is the first supporting sentence in the paragraph?

    ____ **A.** 1   ____ **C.** 3

    ____ **B.** 2   ____ **D.** 7

3. Which is the last supporting sentence in the paragraph?

    ____ **A.** 2   ____ **C.** 6

    ____ **B.** 4   ____ **D.** 7

4. Which sentence is not about the main idea?

    ____ **A.** 3   ____ **C.** 5

    ____ **B.** 4   ____ **D.** 6

PART 4: WRITING

A Paragraph (20 minutes)

Write about something you own that you would never want to lose. Explain why.

- The topic sentence should give the main idea.
- Include sentences to support and explain the topic sentence.
- Use the vocabulary and grammar from Unit 4.

Unit 4 Vocabulary Words			
antique	educational	items	sentimental
collect	favorite	possess	valuable
condition	history	rare	worth
Unit 4 Grammar: The Simple Present			
• Dan *has* a big collection of stamps.			

Achievement Tests
Unit 5

Name: _____

Date: _____

PART 1: READING

1.1 *Read the beginning of an article. Check (✔) the best prediction of what the reading is about. There is only one right answer.*

Teenagers from more than 30 suburban high schools are in Quixote Quest. The teens volunteer in different ways. Some help at-risk teens and teach them about the dangers of drugs.

_____ **A.** teenagers who have troubles

_____ **B.** teenagers who take drugs

_____ **C.** teenagers who do volunteer work

_____ **D.** teenagers who are at-risk students

1.2 *Now read the entire article. Use the information to choose the correct answers.*

Quixote Quest

Are you a teenager living in southern New Jersey? Do you want to make a difference in your community? If you answered "yes," join Quixote Quest!

Teenagers from more than 30 suburban high schools are in Quixote Quest. The teens volunteer in different ways. Some help at-risk teens and teach them about the dangers of drugs. These volunteers try to set good examples by inviting at-risk teens to play sports, take acting classes, and help their community. When kids are involved in their community, they avoid drugs and they do not think about committing crimes and getting into trouble. Other teenagers help senior citizens. They are happy to give senior citizens a hand by carrying their groceries or mowing their lawns.

Chelsea Sanchez, a junior at Washington Township High School, is a three-year member of Quixote Quest. She says, "I love giving support to my community. I take Ms. Reinhold's dog for a walk every morning before school, and I mow Mr. Johnson's lawn. When they are happy, I'm happy."

Marcus Wu, a senior at Eastern High School, is a four-year member of Quixote Quest. "I enjoy volunteering, and I also like spending time with the other teenagers in the group. Everyone has a positive attitude. We treat one another with a lot of respect. My friends in Quixote Quest are my friends for life."

For more information, visit www.mmcgough.homestead.com.

Check (✔) the best answer to complete each sentence.

1. The goal of Quixote Quest is to _____.

   _____ **A.** have fun   _____ **C.** be happy

   _____ **B.** be positive   _____ **D.** help others

2. Quixote Quest teenagers set a good example because they

   _____.

   _____ **A.** are very happy   _____ **C.** study in high school

   _____ **B.** do positive things _____ **D.** take acting classes

3. Only _____ can join Quixote Quest.

   _____ **A.** adults   _____ **C.** teenagers

   _____ **B.** friends   _____ **D.** senior citizens

1.3 *Check (✔) the three words that describe the volunteers in Quixote Quest.*

   _____ **A.** helpful   _____ **D.** supportive

   _____ **B.** at-risk   _____ **E.** respectful

   _____ **C.** different

1.4 *Read the passage from "Urban Angels" in* NorthStar: Reading and Writing 1, *Unit 5. Use the information from this reading and "Quixote Quest" to complete the activity. Not all of the descriptions will be used. The first one has been done for you.*

Urban Angels

A program to address important issues facing teenagers in the U.S.

Urban Angels is a group, or club, for teenagers. The Guardian Angels started Urban Angels to support at-risk teens in the South Bronx in New York City. The Urban Angels Life Skills Program helps teens avoid drugs, gangs, guns, crime, and other trouble. The program wants teens to stay in school and to become positive members of their community. Urban Angels do many things. They have activities after school two days a week and two Saturdays a month. These activities are educational and fun.

Descriptions

A. help senior citizens

~~B. avoid drugs~~

C. support at-risk teens

D. take dogs for walks

E. are positive people

F. have teenage members

Ways Quixote Quest and Urban Angels Are Similar
B
1.
2.
3.

PART 2: VOCABULARY

2.1 *Read the newsletter about Quixote Quest. Use the words from the box to fill in the blanks. Not all of the words will be used.*

avoid   crime   learn   positive   role model   support   teenagers   urban

We are proud of Quixote Quest and we _____ the members'
                                              1.
hard work. The Quixote Quest members help lower _____ in
                                                        2.
our community. They are a _____ influence on young children.
                                3.
They teach children how to play sports, and the children _____
                                                                 4.
quickly. Each person in Quixote Quest is a _____ for children in
                                                  5.
our community.

2.2 *Read the letter to the editor. Use the words from the box to fill in the blanks. Not all of the words will be used.*

fall through the cracks	community	join	teenagers
give someone a hand	members	set a good example	urban

March 18, 2008

Dear Editor,

I live in the South Bronx. The Urban Angels have been helping other

_____ stay out of trouble. They are wonderful members
                      1.

of the _____. I hope other young adults _____
               2.   **3.**

the Urban Angels. The Urban Angels have _____ for
                                                      4.

others. We should not let this program just _____. Please
                                                        5.

support the Urban Angels.

Sincerely,
Mr. Eric Hines

PART 3: SKILLS FOR WRITING

3.1 *Reread the letter to the editor in Part 2.2. Then answer the questions.*

   1. When was the letter written? _____

   2. What is the author asking for? _____

   3. What is the name of the author? _____

3.2 *Complete each sentence with **he**, **him**, or **his**.*

   1. Marcus Wu joined Quixote Quest when _____ was just 13 years old.

   2. It was _____ dream to help others in the community.

   3. Now everyone in the city knows _____.

   4. _____ is always smiling and has a lot of friends.

   5. There should be more teenagers like _____.

3.3 *Read the statements and examples. Rewrite each statement and example in one or two complete sentences. Introduce the examples with the phrase in parentheses.*

1. **Statement:**   Guardian Angels work in urban areas.

   Examples: New York City, Tokyo, and London

   _____

   _____ (such as)

2. **Statement:**   Urban Angels help their communities.

   Example: They clean up parks and help homeless people.

   _____

   _____ (for example)

PART 4: WRITING

A Letter to the Editor (20 minutes)

Reread "Quixote Quest." Then write a one-paragraph letter to the editor about why you support Quixote Quest.

- Use information from the story in Part 1.2.
- Say who you are.
- Give examples to support your reasons.
- Use correct letter format.
- Use the vocabulary and grammar from Unit 5.

Unit 5 Vocabulary Words			
avoid	join	respect	support
crime	members	role models	teenagers
give someone a hand	positive	set a good example	urban
Unit 5 Grammar: Pronouns and Possessive Adjectives			
• *She* saves *her* money.			

PART 1: READING

1.1 *Read the beginning of a letter. Check (✔) the best prediction of what the reading is about. There is only one right answer.*

I just joined Netflix, and it's great! I go online and choose the DVDs that I want. There are more than 90,000 DVDs to choose from. That's more than you can find at Captain Video or at any other video store. Then Netflix's employees mail the DVDs to me. They are really quick. I get the DVDs one or two days later. Netflix really values its customers. Delivery is free . . .

_____ **A.** Captain Video compared to Netflix

_____ **B.** DVDs available from Netflix

_____ **C.** the benefits of Netflix

_____ **D.** online shopping

1.2 *Now read the entire letter. Use the information to choose the correct answers.*

Netflix Is Great!

Dear Katie,

I have to tell you about Netflix. I just joined Netflix, and it's great! I go online and choose the DVDs that I want. There are more than 90,000 DVDs to choose from. That's more than you can find at Captain Video or at any other video store. Then Netflix's employees mail the DVDs to me. They are really quick. I get the DVDs one or two days later. Netflix really values its customers. Delivery is free, and I can get discounts with coupons, too.

Netflix offers so many benefits. Obviously, I save a lot of time and money with Netflix. Also, I can keep the DVDs as long as I want. When I'm done, I put the DVDs in the mail. I don't even have to pay postage. It's so easy.

I think that Netflix is going to compete with all of the video stores because there are many people who are going to become loyal to Netflix. People will stop going to regular video stores and start using Netflix. The owners of regular video stores will start to worry. Do you remember the little barbershop that was on Main Street? It closed when a bigger barbershop opened up down the road. I think Captain Video will close too because Netflix will become very popular.

So, are you going to join Netflix?

See you soon!

Danielle

Check (✔) the best answer to complete each sentence.

1. Netflix customers get their DVDs _____.

   ____ **A.** at Captain Video

   ____ **B.** at the barbershop

   ____ **C.** in the mail

   ____ **D.** at a video store

2. The little barbershop closed because the customers _____.

   ____ **A.** began to worry

   ____ **B.** didn't like Main Street

   ____ **C.** wanted more videos

   ____ **D.** went to the bigger shop

3. Netflix delivery is very _____.

   ____ **A.** cheap

   ____ **B.** expensive

   ____ **C.** fast

   ____ **D.** slow

4. Danielle is trying to convince Katie to _____.

   ____ **A.** join Captain Video

   ____ **B.** join Netflix

   ____ **C.** leave Captain Video

   ____ **D.** leave Netflix

1.3 *Check (✔) the two main ideas that are true.*

   ____ **A.** Netflix offers more benefits than Captain Video.

   ____ **B.** Captain Video offers more DVDs than Netflix.

   ____ **C.** Netflix is a video store on Main Street.

   ____ **D.** Netflix competes for video customers.

   ____ **E.** Captain Video will become more popular.

1.4 *Read the passage from "The Death of the Family-Owned Video Store?" in NorthStar: Reading and Writing 1, Unit 6. Use the information from this reading and "Netflix Is Great!" to complete the activity. The first one has been done for you.*

The Death of the Family-Owned Video Store?

You, our loyal customers, know the benefits Captain Video offers. They are:

- Selection—We have more movies than other video stores in Stamford. We have more than 15,000 DVDs and video games. We are always adding more.
- Service—The employees at Captain Video love movies and know a lot about them, so we can give personal service to all our customers.
- Prices—Because of competition with Blockbuster, we had to increase our prices a little. But we still have great discounts. We also have longer rental times on most DVDs and games.

	Captain Video	Netflix	Both
Has employees			✓
1. Has the larger selection of videos			
2. Gives discounts to customers			
3. Is a business in Stamford			

PART 2: VOCABULARY

2.1 *Use the words from the box to fill in the blanks. Not all of the words will be used.*

barbershop	customers	online	service
coupons	loyal	owners	video store

1. Captain Video is losing some of its local _____.

2. They are no longer _____ customers of the store.

3. Many people have gone from Captain Video to another _____.

4. People want better benefits, such as mail-in _____.

5. Netflix has cheap DVDs and 24-hour customer _____.

2.2 *Complete the sentences with the correct word form: verb (v.), noun (n.), or adjective (adj.). Check (✔) the answer.*

1. Most customers like to receive _____.

_____ **A.** discount (v.)

_____ **B.** discount (n.)

_____ **C.** discounts (n.)

_____ **D.** discounted (adj.)

2. Businesses need to _____ for their customers.

_____ **A.** compete (v.)

_____ **B.** competition (n.)

_____ **C.** competitor (n.)

_____ **D.** competitive (adj.)

3. Captain Video hires _____ from the local community.

_____ **A.** employ (v.)

_____ **B.** employer (n.)

_____ **C.** employees (n.)

_____ **D.** employable (adj.)

4. It is very difficult to _____ a video store.

_____ **A.** own (v.)

_____ **B.** owner (n.)

_____ **C.** ownership (n.)

_____ **D.** own (adj.)

5. But having a business can also be _____.

_____ **A.** benefit (v.)

_____ **B.** benefit (n.)

_____ **C.** benefits (n.)

_____ **D.** beneficial (adj.)

PART 3: SKILLS FOR WRITING

3.1 *Look at the map. Then circle the correct word or phrase in parentheses to complete each sentence. The first one has been done for you.*

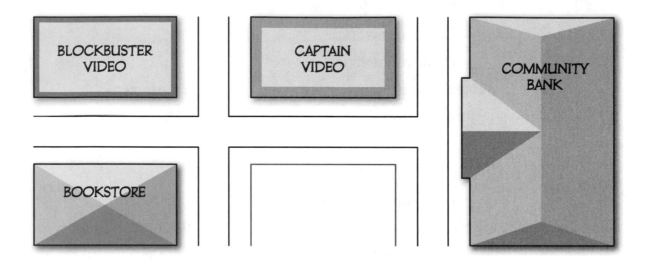

There is nothing (across from / (around the corner from)) Community Bank.

1. Blockbuster Video is (next to / in front of) Captain Video.

2. Captain Video is (between / on) Blockbuster Video and Community Bank.

3. Blockbuster Video is (behind / on the left of) the map.

4. Community Bank is (on the right of / around the corner from) the map.

5. The bookstore is (between / across from) Blockbuster Video.

3.2 *Complete the conversation with **is**, **are**, **isn't**, or **aren't**. One answer is already given.*

FAITH: Hey Kim. ____Is____ there a bank nearby?

KIM: Yeah. There _____ two banks down the street.
  1.

FAITH: Great! There _____ any banks by my house, so I come to the city.
  2.

KIM: There _____ a restaurant next to the bank, if you want to eat.
  3.

FAITH: There _____? OK, I will meet you there after I go to the bank.
  4.

KIM: Let's walk together. There _____ plenty of time.
  5.

PART 4: WRITING

A Description of a Place (20 minutes)

Write a one-paragraph description of a place you see every day.
- Describe the place in detail: How does it look and feel?
- Use space description: Where is it?
- Tell what you like or don't like about the place.
- Use the vocabulary and grammar from Unit 6.

Unit 6 Vocabulary Words			
benefit	customers	loyal	selection
compete	discount	online	service
coupons	employees	owner	store
Unit 6 Grammar: *There is / There are*			
• ***There is*** a new store next to the bank. • ***There are*** many new jobs available at the store.			

PART 1: READING

1.1 *Read part of a story. Check (✔) the best prediction of what the reading is about. There is only one right answer.*

Airplanes were popular in World War I. A Canadian named Billy Bishop was a pilot in the war. He had 72 victories in the war. Ten years later, Charles Lindbergh, a handsome and adventurous 25-year-old pilot, entered a flying contest. The pilots in the contest had to fly alone across the Atlantic Ocean. Lindbergh did it, and he set the record for the longest non-stop flight.

_____ **A.** airplanes   _____ **C.** the Atlantic Ocean

_____ **B.** contests   _____ **D.** World War I

1.2 *Now read the entire story. Use the information to choose the correct answers.*

The History of Flight

Many people think the history of flight started in the twentieth century. However, it began even earlier. In 1783, two brothers, Joseph and Jacques Motgolfier, invented the first hot air balloon. In 1891, the German engineer Otto Lilienthal constructed a glider that carried a person in the air. Then in 1903, Orville and Wilbur Wright made a better glider and called it the Flyer. The Flyer took off for the first time on December 17, 1903. The media took pictures and wrote articles. The Flyer became the world's first real airplane.

Airplanes were popular in World War I. A Canadian named Billy Bishop was a pilot in the war. He had 72 victories in the war. People called him a hero. Ten years later, Charles Lindbergh, a handsome and adventurous 25-year-old pilot, entered a flying contest. The pilots in the contest had to fly alone across the Atlantic Ocean. Lindbergh did it, and he set the record for the longest non-stop flight.

Engineers made airplanes bigger and better. People could fly around the world. NASA, the United States' space program, wanted people to fly to space. In 1961, the American Alan Shepard piloted the first flight into space.

Check (✔) the best answer to complete each sentence.

1. The first airplanes were _____ than they are today.

_____ **A.** better   _____ **C.** faster

_____ **B.** bigger   _____ **D.** simpler

2. The Wright Brothers made the first real _____.

   _____ **A.** airplane   _____ **C.** hot air balloon

   _____ **B.** glider   _____ **D.** rocket

3. The history of flight began _____ the twentieth century.

   _____ **A.** after   _____ **C.** before

   _____ **B.** around   _____ **D.** during

1.3 *Fill in the blanks using the correct numbers from the reading.*

   1. The Motgolfier brothers invented the first hot air balloon in
      _____.

   2. The first glider was constructed in _____.

   3. Billy Bishop had _____ victories in World War I.

1.4 *Read "Charles Lindbergh's Life" from* NorthStar: Reading and Writing 1, *Unit 7.
Use the information from this reading and "The History of Flight" to number the
events in the order they happened. The first one is numbered zero.*

Charles Lindbergh's Life

May 27, 1929	Lindbergh married Anne Morrow.
April 1935	Lindbergh invented an "artificial heart."
Dec. 21, 1935	Lindbergh, his wife, and their second son, Jon, moved to England to protect themselves from the media.
Late 1930s–early 1940s	He visited airplane factories in Germany.
1954	He won the Pulitzer Prize for *The Spirit of St. Louis*, a book about his flight.
Late 1960s–early 1970s	He became an environmentalist.

   _____ **A.** Lindbergh visited Germany.

   _____ **B.** The first pilot flew into space.

   _____ **C.** Charles Lindbergh's family moved to England.

   _0_ **D.** The Flyer made its first flight.

PART 2: VOCABULARY

2.1 *Use the words from the box to fill in the blanks. Not all of the words will be used.*

adventurous	contest	kidnapped	pilot
airplane	flight	media	set a record

1. Amelia Earhart was the first female _____ to fly across the Atlantic Ocean.

2. She _____ when she flew solo across the Atlantic Ocean.

3. Earhart disappeared during her last _____ over the Pacific.

4. No one knows what happened to the _____ that was lost.

5. Amelia Earhart was an _____ pilot.

2.2 *Read the sentences. Check (✔) the word that is NOT close in meaning to the boldfaced word. There is only one right answer.*

1. The **cost** for the flight is not very much.

   _____ **A.** expense   _____ **C.** price

   _____ **B.** money   _____ **D.** wait

2. Workers **construct** large planes in France.

   _____ **A.** build   _____ **C.** make

   _____ **B.** destroy   _____ **D.** produce

3. In 1935, Amelia Earhart **took off** from Hawaii.

   _____ **A.** arrived   _____ **C.** flew

   _____ **B.** departed   _____ **D.** left

4. Many people thought Lindbergh was very **handsome**.

   _____ **A.** attractive   _____ **C.** good-looking

   _____ **B.** cute   _____ **D.** ugly

5. He was **well-known** all over the world.

   _____ **A.** famous   _____ **C.** liked

   _____ **B.** hated   _____ **D.** popular

PART 3: SKILLS FOR WRITING

3.1 *Complete the sentences in time order. Use the information from the box.*

> I wait by the door for my dad.
>
> I get dressed and put on my shoes.
>
> I wake up and eat breakfast.
>
> he picks me up in his car.
>
> my mother gives me my books.

Every day of the week is the same.

1. First, _____

2. Then _____

3. Next, _____

4. Later, _____

5. Finally, _____

My dad drives me to school every day!

3.2 *Read the paragraph. Write the past tense form of the verbs in parentheses. The first one has been done for you.*

Charles Lindbergh _____had_____ an amazing life. He _____ from
            (have)   1. (fly)

North America to Europe without stopping. Then he _____ home
                                                2. (return)

some time later. He is one of my heroes! Lindbergh also _____ the
                                                      3. (create)

first artificial heart. A person needs a lot of knowledge and time to do that. I

am sure it _____ him many years to make it. I _____ flying
            4. (take)   5. (try)

once too, but I will never be Charles Lindbergh.

PART 4: WRITING

An Autobiography (20 minutes)

Write a paragraph about an exciting adventure that you have had.

- Include a topic sentence.
- Write events in the order they happened.
- Use time order words.
- Include a timeline that describes the adventure.
- Use the vocabulary and grammar from Unit 7.

Unit 7 Vocabulary Words			
adventurous	cost	hero	simple
constructed	flight	media	took off
contest	handsome	pilots	well-known
Unit 7 Grammar: The Simple Past			
• Dan *received* an invitation. • He *went* to Canada by bus.			

Name: _____

Date: _____

PART 1: READING

1.1 *Read the beginning of a letter. Check (✔) the best prediction of what the reading is about. There is only one right answer.*

Heavy traffic is a big problem in New York City. It takes a long time, sometimes an hour, to drive across Manhattan. Drivers are always in a rush, and when they are, they are dangerous. New York City has the highest number of pedestrian deaths and injuries in the country.

_____ **A.** living in New York City

_____ **B.** walking in New York City

_____ **C.** solving the traffic problem in New York City

_____ **D.** solving the pedestrian death problem in New York City

1.2 *Now read the entire letter. Use the information to choose the correct answers.*

Traffic in New York City

From: Advisor to New York City Mayor
To: Traffic Solutions Committee, New York, NY
Subject: Traffic Proposal

Heavy traffic is a big problem in New York City. It takes a long time, sometimes an hour, to drive across Manhattan. Drivers are always in a rush, and when they are, they are dangerous. New York City has the highest number of pedestrian deaths and injuries in the country.

    I am proposing three changes. First, we will have bike lanes on many streets so bicyclists will be safer. Some people who commute by car will start to ride their bikes to work because they will feel safe.

    Second, we will have a "Deduct-a-Ride" program. Commuters will pay lower taxes if they take public buses, trains, and subways. We will add bus routes and train stations closer to people's homes. Public transportation will be convenient. In addition, we will add an express subway line to get people to work on time.

    Finally, we will have a traffic tax for people who drive in the city. The tax will be $8 per car. People will take public transportation instead of paying the tax. City residents will be happy because there will be less traffic on their streets.

(continued on next page)

Please consider these solutions to the city's traffic problems. Our next meeting is December 4.

Sincerely,
Advisor to New York City Mayor

Check (✔) the best answer to complete each sentence.

1. Traffic is a big problem in New York City because _____.

   _____ **A.** so many people drive there

   _____ **B.** there are no buses and trains

   _____ **C.** bicycling is not allowed

   _____ **D.** people pay traffic taxes

2. It often takes _____ to drive through Manhattan.

   _____ **A.** eight minutes

   _____ **B.** one hour

   _____ **C.** two hours

   _____ **D.** one day

3. The advisor to the mayor has solutions to _____ in New York City.

   _____ **A.** decrease pedestrians

   _____ **B.** decrease traffic

   _____ **C.** increase cars

   _____ **D.** increase deaths

4. All of the following are solutions to the traffic problems *except* _____.

   _____ **A.** affordable cars

   _____ **B.** bike lanes

   _____ **C.** a commuter program

   _____ **D.** a traffic tax

5. People will pay _____ dollars per car to drive into New York City.

    ____ **A.** three

    ____ **B.** four

    ____ **C.** eight

    ____ **D.** ten

6. Pedestrian deaths occur in New York when people drive

    _____.

    ____ **A.** dangerously

    ____ **B.** carefully

    ____ **C.** safely

    ____ **D.** slowly

1.3 *Read the passage from "Looking for Traffic Solutions" in* NorthStar: Reading and Writing 1, *Unit 8. Use the information from this reading and "Traffic in New York City" to complete the activity. One solution has two locations. The first one has been done for you.*

Looking for Traffic Solutions

- Atlanta, Georgia, has an online traffic map. The map shows commuters where there is heavy traffic. Drivers can check the traffic on their computers at home.

- The State of Connecticut has a "Deduct-a-Ride" program. Commuters save money if they don't use their cars. They pay lower taxes when they use public buses and trains.

- Bangkok, Thailand, has a skytrain. It's like the subway but not underground. It is about 14 miles (23 km) long. It is clean, fast, and on time.

Solutions	Atlanta	Connecticut	Bangkok	New York City
Online traffic map	✓			
Skytrain				
Deduct-a-Ride				

PART 2: VOCABULARY

2.1 *Use the words from the box to fill in the blanks. Not all of the words will be used.*

convenient	heavy traffic	lanes	on time	residents
commute	helicopter	meeting	pedestrian	solutions

I never get to work _____ because there is so much
1.

_____. The city needs to develop some good
2.

_____ to the traffic problems. Last week, our city had a
3.

_____ about decreasing traffic. Some people had great ideas,
4.

but the ideas were not _____. I believe people should just walk
5.

to work or take the bus. Maybe some people can even _____ to
6.

work with other employees.

2.2 *Complete the paragraph using **get**, **go**, or **take**. Use the correct form of the word.*

I don't like to _____ my car to work. So, each morning I take the bus
1.

to _____ to work. After I leave the house, I _____ down the
2.   **3.**

street and wait at the bus stop. It's safe and I always _____ to work
4.

on time.

PART 3: SKILLS FOR WRITING

3.1 *Read the paragraph. Find the comparative adjectives and write them on the lines.*

Driving in New York City is easier than driving in London. In London, it is
more crowded and it is noisier. People and cars make lots of noise. It is less
expensive to drive in New York City than London. Driving is simpler in New
York City. However, it is more fun to live in London!

_____*easier than*_____

1. _____

2. _____

3. _____

4. _____

5. _____

3.2 *Put the sentences in order. The first one has been done for you.*

(**A**) Third, people can do work on their way to work. (**B**) People love to use public transportation in New York City for many reasons. (**C**) We should all think seriously about using public transportation in the future. (**D**) Second, there are a lot of train and bus stops, which makes traveling convenient. (**E**) First, it is less expensive than driving a car. (**F**) Finally, taking public transportation helps to reduce pollution from all of the cars.

       __B__

1. ____   4. ____

2. ____   5. ____

3. ____

PART 4: WRITING

A Comparison and Contrast Paragraph (20 minutes)

Compare and contrast two kinds of transportation.

- Give the main idea in your topic sentence.
- Describe how the kinds of transportation are similar and different.
- Use transition words to put your reasons in order.
- Use the vocabulary and grammar from Unit 8.

Unit 8 Vocabulary Words			
committee	lanes	pedestrian	subway
commute	meeting	resident	take (time)
convenient	on time	solution	traffic
Unit 8 Grammar: Comparative Adjectives			
• The subway is *bigger* and *busier* here.			

PART 1: READING

1.1 *Read the beginning of a letter. Check (✔) the best prediction of what the reading is about. There is only one right answer.*

I am an only child. I grew up without any siblings. I wanted my mom to get pregnant and give me a younger brother or sister. I was lonely. . . . I knew from a very young age that I wanted to raise a big family someday.

_____ **A.** being lonely

_____ **B.** getting along with siblings

_____ **C.** advantages of being an only child

_____ **D.** advantages of a large family

1.2 *Now read the entire letter. Use the information to choose the correct answers.*

Only and Lonely

Dear Editor:

An article in your last issue said that more parents should have only one child. I disagree.

I am an only child. I grew up without any siblings. I wanted my mom to get pregnant and give me a younger brother or sister. I was lonely.

I felt like the black sheep at school because all of my friends had siblings. They always had someone to play with. I was jealous, and I hated being different. My mom told me that it was good to be unique. She told me that I had more privacy than kids with siblings. My dad said I was lucky because I didn't have to share my bedroom or my toys.

I knew from a very young age that I wanted to raise a big family someday. Now I am 40 years old, and I am the mother of three boys and a girl. I am very happy, but I worry a lot. I want to protect my children and make sure that they are safe. Raising four kids is a challenge, but my family and friends help. My mom babysits, and my friends with older children donate their kids' old clothes to my kids.

Please don't tell your readers that it is better to have only one child. My childhood was quiet and sad without siblings.

Sincerely,
Carrie Kline

Check (✔) the best answer to complete each sentence.

1. The author felt that she was different because she _____.

      _____ **A.** shared her toys   _____ **C.** had more privacy

      _____ **B.** had no siblings   _____ **D.** raised a big family

2. Carrie Kline's dad told her she was _____ because she did not have to share her things.

      _____ **A.** sad   _____ **C.** worried

      _____ **B.** lucky   _____ **D.** happy

3. Carrie Kline now has a _____ family.

      _____ **A.** big   _____ **C.** quiet

      _____ **B.** small   _____ **D.** lucky

4. Carrie Kline has _____ children.

      _____ **A.** two   _____ **C.** four

      _____ **B.** three   _____ **D.** five

5. The author is _____ having several children.

      _____ **A.** against   _____ **C.** opposed to

      _____ **B.** for   _____ **D.** unsure of

6. Having children is _____ for Kline.

      _____ **A.** challenging   _____ **C.** lonely

      _____ **B.** easy   _____ **D.** safe

1.3 *Read the passage from "Full House" in* NorthStar: Reading and Writing 1, *Unit 9. Use the information from this reading and "Only and Lonely" to complete the activity. The first one has been done for you.*

Full House

The kids are sometimes noisy, but there is also a lot of laughter. But Bobbi and Kenny love all eight children. Each one is unique:

- Mikayla is one year older than the septuplets. Sometimes she feels jealous, but not often. She is a good big sister.
- Kenny Jr. was the first septuplet. His nickname is "Bert." He is energetic.

(continued on next page)

- Alexis has the best smile. She likes to listen to violin music in her room.
- Natalie is dramatic. When she was little, she cried about many things. But she is a good girl.
- Kelsey is very friendly. She likes to talk to people. She talks a lot.
- Nathan is shy and likes to laugh. He likes to play with the other kids.
- Brandon likes "army" things. He likes to play outside.
- Joel likes to read. He also thinks about things carefully.

Statements	Mikayla	Carrie	Neither
She was an only child.		✓	
1. She is a big sister.			
2. She has three brothers and one sister.			
3. She thinks having one child is good.			

PART 2: VOCABULARY

2.1 *Check (✔) the best answer to complete each sentence.*

1. To **raise a family** means to _____.

_____ **A.** do fun things with your family

_____ **B.** keep your family happy

_____ **C.** keep the family challenged

_____ **D.** take care of the family

2. If someone wants **privacy**, he or she wants to _____.

_____ **A.** talk with others

_____ **B.** have lots of friends

_____ **C.** be left alone

_____ **D.** be helped by others

3. If a person is the **black sheep**, that person is _____.

_____ **A.** afraid of others

_____ **B.** different from others

_____ **C.** more sad than others

_____ **D.** the same as others

4. To **protect** something means to keep it _____.

_____ **A.** safe

_____ **B.** quiet

_____ **C.** happy

_____ **D.** clean

5. A person who **grew up** in a city _____.

_____ **A.** had children in that city

_____ **B.** lived there as a child

_____ **C.** moved there after school

_____ **D.** visited the city as a child

2.2 *Use the words from the box to fill in the blanks. Not all of the words will be used.*

an only child	raise a family	sibling rivalry	the middle child
grew up	runs in the family	the black sheep	took after

I don't have any siblings. As _____, I could do anything I
                                                    1.
wanted. I was lucky. I didn't have to worry about any _____.
                                                                    2.
     I have my mother's red hair. She said that I _____ her. I
                                                                3.
knew that I wanted to _____ one day. Now I have three
                                    4.
children. They all have red hair. I guess it _____.
                                                            5.

T-45

PART 3: SKILLS FOR WRITING

3.1 *Complete the sentences using **should** or **shouldn't**.*

1. Too many children are not good. I think people _____ have small families.

2. That's a bad idea. We _____ listen to such bad ideas.

3. Parents do not talk with their children enough. I think they _____ talk more.

4. I think it's wrong to spank children. Parents _____ spank their children.

5. Kids have a lot of energy. They _____ learn to play outside.

3.2 *Read the interview. Then answer the questions. Check (✔) the correct answers.*

ANNOUNCER: How many children do you have, Carrie?
CARRIE: I have four kids.
ANNOUNCER: Wow!
CARRIE: I love kids!
ANNOUNCER: Do you think people should have big families?
CARRIE: In my opinion, people should have big families. One reason I think that big families are great is that there is always someone to talk to. I knew from a young age that I wanted to raise a big family. You need a lot of money to raise children. Another reason to have a big family is that children are great fun! They make life very enjoyable. For these reasons, I think everyone should have a big family.
ANNOUNCER: What do YOU think?

1. What is the first follow-up question in the interview?

_____ **A.** How many children do you have, Carrie?

_____ **B.** Why?

_____ **C.** Do you think people should have big families?

_____ **D.** What do YOU think?

2. What is the opinion in Carrie's answer to the second question?

_____ **A.** Carrie loves kids.

_____ **B.** Carrie knew from a young age that she wanted to raise a big family.

_____ **C.** Carrie has four kids.

_____ **D.** People should have big families.

3. Which sentence does not belong?

_____ **A.** Another reason to have a big family is that children are great fun!

_____ **B.** You need a lot of money to raise children.

_____ **C.** One reason I think that big families are great is that there is always someone to talk to.

_____ **D.** They make life very enjoyable.

4. What is the concluding sentence in Carrie's answer to the second question?

_____ **A.** I have four kids.

_____ **B.** They make life very enjoyable.

_____ **C.** For these reasons, I think everyone should have a big family.

_____ **D.** In my opinion, people should have big families.

5. What type of concluding sentence is used?

_____ **A.** opinion

_____ **B.** repetition

_____ **C.** prediction

_____ **D.** follow-up question

PART 4: WRITING

An Opinion Paragraph (20 minutes)

Write a paragraph on your opinion about this topic: Parents with little money should have only one child.

- Use information from "Only and Lonely."
- Give reasons for your opinion.
- Use opinion expressions.
- Write a concluding sentence that restates your opinion or makes a prediction.
- Use the vocabulary and grammar from Unit 9.

Unit 9 Vocabulary Words			
challenge	jealous	privacy	siblings
donate	laughter	protect	the black sheep
grow up	pregnant	raise a family	unique
Unit 9 Grammar: *Should*			
• We ***should*** eat dinner together.			

Achievement Tests
Unit 10

Name: _____

Date: _____

PART 1: READING

1.1 *Read the passage from a newsletter. Check (✔) the best prediction of what the reading is about. There is only one right answer.*

Most high school seniors are going to college after they graduate. Brett Shaw won't be one of them. Shaw, our school's best basketball star, is going to play in the NBA for the New York Knicks. I don't think it's a good idea to skip college and join the professional basketball league early.

_____ **A.** choosing sports and not going to college

_____ **B.** earning money after college

_____ **C.** playing in the NBA

_____ **D.** graduating from high school

1.2 *Now read the entire newsletter. Use the information to choose the correct answers.*

Sports Instead of College?

Most high school seniors are going to college after they graduate. Brett Shaw won't be one of them. Shaw, our school's best basketball star, is going to play in the NBA for the New York Knicks.

I don't think it's a good idea to skip college and join the professional basketball league early. Kwame Brown, a professional basketball player, did that. He had a lot of talent, but he was not as mature as the older players. He did not know how to be a team player. He wanted to be the best, so he hogged the ball. Often, instead of passing the ball to a teammate, Brown held on to it. He wanted to score all the points and be the most famous. As a result, his team lost a lot of games. Other players as well as fans made a lot of rude comments about Brown. Brown couldn't deal with it, so he stopped going to practice. His coach decided that Brown should not be allowed to call all the shots, and the coach suspended Brown from the playoffs.

Everyone expected Kwame Brown to be the next Michael Jordan. However, Brown disappointed his fans because he was not mature enough to deal with all the fame and money. All great athletes should go to college first. When they graduate, they will have an education and be mentally prepared for life as a professional athlete.

(continued on next page)

Check (✔) the best answer to complete each sentence.

1. Brown's team lost a lot of games because Brown _____.

    _____ **A.** could not call the shots

    _____ **B.** did not go to college

    _____ **C.** was not a good teammate

    _____ **D.** was not liked by the fans

2. Brown was suspended from _____.

    _____ **A.** college

    _____ **B.** high school

    _____ **C.** the playoffs

    _____ **D.** the practices

3. Athletes are more _____ prepared after graduating from college.

    _____ **A.** mentally

    _____ **B.** physically

    _____ **C.** emotionally

    _____ **D.** financially

4. _____ people are better professional athletes.

    _____ **A.** Young

    _____ **B.** Rude

    _____ **C.** Old

    _____ **D.** Mature

1.3 *Check (✔) the two main ideas from the reading.*

    _____ **1.** Brown suspended his teammate from the playoffs.

    _____ **2.** It is difficult to be a professional athlete.

    _____ **3.** An education cannot prepare a professional athlete.

    _____ **4.** Brown did not like players who hogged the ball.

    _____ **5.** Some young athletes are not mature enough for life as a professional athlete.

1.4 *Read the passage from "Bram Tarek: Young Basketball Star Says 'No' to the Pros"*
in NorthStar: Reading and Writing 1, Unit 10. *Use the information from this*
reading and "Sports Instead of College?" to complete the activity. Not all of the
statements will be used. The first one has been done for you.

Bram Tarek: Young Basketball Star Says "No" to the Pros

NICOLA QUINN: Bram, everyone expected you to join the NBA this year.
Why did you decide to finish college first?

BRAM TAREK: Well, I planned to join the NBA as soon as I was old
enough. But then I met older basketball players. They said I
should stay in college.

NICOLA QUINN: Who did you talk to?

BRAM TAREK: Several basketball players. But Kareem Abdul-Jabbar
probably helped me the most. He is my biggest basketball
hero. He's the greatest. But, in his day, all players had to go
to college before joining the NBA. Today it's different. He
said college helped the players to become more mature—
intellectually and physically.

NICOLA QUINN: But what about the money? How can you say "no" to all that
money?

BRAM TAREK: Oh, that was really hard! Kareem helped a lot. He really
taught me that money is not #1.

A. was not able to earn millions after high school

B. ~~talked to a star athlete about college~~

C. thought he was better than Kareem Abdul-Jabbar

D. thought a college education was not important

E. wasn't allowed to call the shots

F. was going to play for the New York Knicks

	Advantages	Disadvantages
Bram Tarek	B	2.
Kwame Brown	1.	3.

PART 2: VOCABULARY

2.1 *Use the words from the box to fill in the blanks. Not all of the words will be used.*

a basketball player	calling the shots	get on the ball	hogging the ball
a team player	deal with	go to college	join the NBA

Kwame Brown was not _____. Brown's coach wanted to start

                                1.

_____, but Brown could not _____ it. His

            2.   **3.**

coach warned him to _____ or the team would not let him

                                       4.

play. After that time, Brown stopped _____, and the team

                                              5.

started to win games.

2.2 *Read the sentences. Circle the one word or phrase that makes sense.*

1. Kwame Brown (had a lot of / gained a lot of / made a lot of) talent in basketball.

2. (After graduating / Before graduating / While graduating) from high school, some athletes go to college.

3. Fans make rude comments (about / on / in) athletes all the time.

4. Bram Tarek wants to become (more / less / greater) mature in college.

5. Coaches are paid to (break the decisions / make the decisions / take the decisions) about their team.

PART 3: SKILLS FOR WRITING

3.1 *Write the correct word or words to complete the sentences. The first one has been done for you.*

Casual advice: Fans _____*can*_____ cheer for the athletes they like

                               (can / should)

best.

1. Specific advice: Bram Tarek _____ thank Kareem Abdul-

                                        (should / has to)

Jabbar for his advice.

2. Specific advice: Fans _____ yell at athletes because it is
(had better not / shouldn't)

   rude.

3. Stronger advice: You _____ go to college if you want to
(can / had better)

   do well in professional sports.

4. Stronger advice: You _____ miss practice if you want to
(had better not / can't)

   play this weekend.

5. The strongest advice: This is the last game of the season. You

   _____ go!
(have to / should)

3.2 *Put the words in order to make sentences.*

1. enough / Kwame Brown / mature / not / was

   _____

2. money / some / too / athletes / much / make

   _____

3. Michael Jordan / very / player / a / basketball / good / was

   _____

4. old / play / too / am / I / to / sports

   _____

5. a / Brown / not / team / was / very / player / good

   _____

PART 4: WRITING

A Letter of Advice (20 minutes)

Write one paragraph of advice in a letter to an athlete who does not want to go to college.

- Use information from "Sports Instead of College?"
- Show that you understand the problem.
- Give a reason for your advice.
- Use the appropriate advice language.
- At the end, offer to help or give a final comment.
- Use the vocabulary and grammar from Unit 10.

Unit 10 Vocabulary Words			
be a team player	comments	get on the ball	mature
call the shots	deal with	graduate	responsible
coach	expect	hog the ball	talent
Unit 10 Grammar: *Very, Too,* and *Enough*			
<ul><li>Athletes are **very** gifted people.</li><li>The youngest player was not mature **enough**.</li><li>Some athletes are **too** old to play.</li></ul>			

Achievement Tests Answer Key

UNIT 1

1.1

C

1.2

1. D   2. A

1.3

A, B, C, F

1.4

1. Both 2. Europa Pages   3. MySpace

2.1

1. meet   6. volunteers
2. chat   7. peace
3. community   8. personal
4. advice   9. goals
5. safe   10. laugh

3.1

1. Europa Pages   3. are   5. 4
2. 1   4. 4

3.2

1. Who has to pay for Europa Pages?
2. Is Keyana Campbell learning Spanish?
3. Do you have many friends at Europa Pages?
4. Does the website have volunteers to help?
5. Where are Jacques and Debbie from?

PART 4

Answers will vary. See the scoring rubric on page T-59.

UNIT 2

1.1

C

1.2

1. A   2. D   3. D

1.3

(in any order)
1. feel equal   2. neat   3. increase school spirit

1.4

1. E   2. B   3. D

2.1

1. C   2. A   3. A   4. C   5. B

2.2

1. uniforms   4. comfortable
2. equal   5. fashion
3. wear

3.1

1. C   2. A   3. F

3.2

1. comfortable black wool
2 messy green plaid

3.3

1. will not OR won't   4. will
2. Will   5. will
3. will not OR won't

PART 4

Answers will vary. See the scoring rubric on page T-59.

UNIT 3

1.1

B

1.2

1. D   2. B   3. B

1.3

1. 1949 2. 44   3. 1956

1.4

1. freedom 2. magazines   3. museums

2.1

1. energetic   4. ads
2. graffiti   5. social issues
3. pop

2.2

1. drawing OR drawings   4. social
2. freedom   5. famous
3. dance

3.1

A. 1   B. 3   D. 2

3.2

1. Paul Jackson Pollock visited Los Angeles, California.
2. Haring lived in New York, New York, for several years.

3.3

1. wasn't   4. didn't have
2. had   5. was
3. were

PART 4

Answers will vary. See the scoring rubric on page T-59.

UNIT 4

1.1

A

1.2

1. A   2. C

1.3

1. B   2. C   3. A   4. D

1.4

1. My Secret   2. Both   3. Try a New Career

2.1

1. history OR antiques   4. valuable OR smart
2. antiques OR history   5. educate
3. smart OR valuable

2.2

1. sentimental   4. collector
2. worth   5. items
3. condition

3.1

1. Do   3. have   5. collects
2. need   4. is   6. wants

3.2

1. A   2. B   3. D   4. B

PART 4

Answers will vary. See the scoring rubric on page T-59.

UNIT 5

1.1

C

1.2

1. D   2. B   3. C

1.3

A, D, E

1.4

(in any order)

1. C   2. E   3. F

2.1

1. support   4. learn
2. crime   5. role model
3. positive

2.2

1. teenagers   4. set a good example
2. community   5. fall through the cracks
3. join

3.1

1. March 18, 2008   3. Mr. Eric Hines
2. money OR support

3.2

1. he   2. his   3. him   4. He   5. him

3.3

1. Guardian Angels work in urban areas such as New York City, Tokyo, and London.
2. Urban Angels help their communities. For example, they clean up parks and help homeless people.

PART 4

Answers will vary. See the scoring rubric on page T-59.

UNIT 6

1.1

C

1.2

1. C   2. D   3. C   4. B

1.3

A and D

1.4

1. Netflix   2. Both   3. Captain Video

2.1

1. customers   4. coupons
2. loyal   5. service
3. video store

2.2

1. C   2. A   3. C   4. A   5. D

3.1

1. next to
2. between
3. on the left of
4. on the right of
5. across from

3.2

1. are
2. aren't OR are not
3. is
4. is
5. is

PART 4

Answers will vary. See the scoring rubric on page T-59.

UNIT 7

1.1

A

1.2

1. D   2. A   3. C

1.3

1. 1783   2. 1891   3. 72

1.4

A. 2   **B.** 3   **C.** 1

2.1

1. pilot
2. set a record
3. flight
4. airplane
5. adventurous

2.2

1. D   2. B   3. A   4. D   5. B

3.1

1. I wake up and eat breakfast.
2. I get dressed and put on my shoes.
3. my mother gives me my books.
4. I wait by the door for my dad.
5. he picks me up in his car.

3.2

1. flew
2. returned
3. created
4. took
5. tried

PART 4

Answers will vary. See the scoring rubric on page T-59.

UNIT 8

1.1

C

1.2

1. A   3. B   5. C
2. B   4. A   6. A

1.3

Skytrain: Bangkok
Deduct-a-Ride: Connecticut and New York City

2.1

1. on time
2. heavy traffic
3. solutions
4. meeting
5. convenient
6. commute

2.2

1. take
2. go OR get
3. go
4. get

3.1

1. more crowded
2. noisier
3. less expensive
4. simpler
5. more fun

3.2

1. E   2. D   3. A   4. F   5. C

PART 4

Answers will vary. See the scoring rubric on page T-59.

UNIT 9

1.1

D

1.2

1. B   3. A   5. B
2. B   4. C   6. A

1.3

1. Mikayla   2. Neither   3. Neither

2.1

1. D   2. C   3. B   4. A   5. B

2.2

1. an only child
2. sibling rivalry
3. took after
4. raise a family
5. runs in the family

3.1

1. should
2. shouldn't
3. should
4. shouldn't
5. should

3.2

1. C   2. D   3. B   4. C   5. B

PART 4

Answers will vary. See the scoring rubric on page T-59.

UNIT 10

1.1

A

1.2

1. C   2. C   3. A   4. D

1.3

2 and 5

1.4

1. F   2. A   3. D

2.1

1. a team player
2. calling the shots
3. deal with
4. get on the ball
5. hogging the ball

2.2

1. had a lot of
2. After graduating
3. about
4. more
5. make the decisions

3.1

1. should
2. shouldn't
3. had better
4. had better not
5. have to

3.2

1. Kwame Brown was not mature enough.
2. Some athletes make too much money.
3. Michael Jordan was a very good basketball player.
4. I am too old to play sports.
5. Brown was not a very good team player.

PART 4

Answers will vary. See the scoring rubric on page T-59.

NorthStar 1 Achievement Test Scoring Rubric: Writing

Score	Description
5	A response at this level contains relevant information from the test reading passage; however, the information needs more development. A response at this level is also marked by several of the following: • adequate organization and a somewhat effective attempt to use transition words and phrases to sequence and organize information • more than one paragraph; there is a main idea and multiple supporting sentences • consistent, correct use of subject-verb agreement, pronouns, relative clauses, infinitives, modals, and simple verb tenses • appropriate use of a variety of vocabulary items from the unit • several language errors throughout
4	A response at this level contains some information from the test reading passage and is marked by: • somewhat adequate organization; the writer is just beginning to use transition words to sequence information, but more practice is needed • only one paragraph; there is a simple main idea and several supporting sentences • generally consistent, correct use of subject-verb agreement, pronouns, relative clauses, infinitives, modals, and simple verb tenses • appropriate use of several vocabulary items from the unit • several language errors in paragraph
3	A response at this level contains little information from the test reading passage and is marked by: • somewhat adequate organization of information • several complete sentences; there is a simple main idea and few supporting sentences • generally consistent, correct use of subject-verb agreement, personal pronouns, WH- relative clauses, and simple verb tenses • appropriate use of 1–2 vocabulary items from the unit • numerous language errors per sentence
2	A response at this level contains very little information from the test reading passage and is marked by: • very little organization of information • only a few complete sentences to form a short paragraph; the writer is just beginning to provide a main idea and supporting sentences, but more practice is needed • somewhat consistent, correct use of subject-verb agreement and simple verb tenses • inappropriate use of vocabulary from the unit • numerous language errors per clause
1	A response at this level contains almost no information from the test reading passage and indicates several of the following: • a lack of organization of information • several complete and incomplete sentences; the writer needs to provide a main idea and supporting sentences • a lack of consistent, correct use of subject-verb agreement and simple verb tenses • inappropriate use of vocabulary from the unit • numerous language errors per phrase
0	A response at this level is written in a foreign language, consists of keystroke characters, or is blank.